The Fairy Courts

From Folklore to Fiction

What People Are Saying About

The Fairy Courts

An in depth and detailed history of the lore of fairy courts from early days to today. I'm familiar with this topic but was amazed at how much more I learned from this book.

Catherine Kane, author of *Living in Interesting Times: Practical Energy Work When Times Get Tough* and the Morgan and Sam urban fantasy series

Outstanding in its thoroughness, complexity and clarity, *Fairy Courts* is an invaluable resource for whoever wants to dive deeper into the subject of seelie and unseelie fairy courts whether from scholarly interest or personal spiritual pursuits.

Daniela Simina, author of *Where Fairies Meet: Parallels between Irish and Romanian Fairy Traditions*

Fascinating ... Morgan Daimler's *The Fairy Courts* is a must read for anyone wishing to explore the roots of Scottish folk beliefs around the seelie and unseelie courts. I found myself transported to the Otherworlds of the trooping, solitary, and royal fairies in this captivating book. Highly researched, insightful, and utterly magical.

Melanie Godfrey, author of *Ancient Fayerie* and *The Magic of the Seal*

The Fairy Courts is a wonderfully rich exploration of the concept of Fairy society, across different cultures and encompassing traditional to modern ideas. The author untangles the various sources that shape our understanding of Fairy Courts. Fairy monarchs, hierarchies and social groups come to life, with a nuanced appreciation of both the similarities and differences

across Scottish, Irish and European cultures. Especially fascinating is the insight into how modern literature and gaming have affected our understanding of these things as well as the author's guidelines on Fairy etiquette based on traditional folklore and belief. Deeply informative and highly entertaining!
Geraldine Moorkens Byrne, author of *Dreams of Reality* and *Draíocht Ceoil: The Sound of Magic in Irish Traditions*

Fairies in Scotland are different in some ways. Living in Scotland I have felt a great curiosity to learn about their folklore and spirituality. In my personal work I have connected with local deities, but also with other invisible beings that inhabit these northern lands. I have to say that this book is without a doubt a great gift for anyone who wants to know about Fairy Courts. Morgan synthesizes in a single volume an incredible amount of information about them. Not only is it an exceptional reference book, it clearly explains the concept and structure and differences or similarities with other fairies, in Ireland, Wales, France, Romania or England... Chapter 7 is a gem in itself, in which Morgan shares her tips to "Survive" the Fairy Courts. This is truly, and I repeat myself but it is the truth, an exceptional book and a must read whether you are interested in fairies in general or Scottish folklore.
Ness Bosch, author of *Sacred Bones Magic Bones* and founding member of the Goddess Community Scotland

As ever, Morgan Daimler provides a succinct exploration of an aspect of fairy lore, this time the misunderstood concept of fairy courts. Morgan's approach is both accessible and rooted in extensive research. This is a highly recommended read for anyone interested in fairy lore, or considering using it in their fiction.
Icy Sedgwick, host of the *Fabulous Folklore* podcast

The Fairy Courts

From Folklore to Fiction

Morgan Daimler

London, UK
Washington, DC, USA

First published by Moon Books, 2026
Moon Books is an imprint of Collective Ink Ltd.,
Unit 11, Shepperton House, 89 Shepperton Road, London, N1 3DF
office@collectiveinkbooks.com
www.collectiveinkbooks.com
www.moon-books.net

For distributor details and how to order please visit the 'Ordering' section on our website.

ISBN: 978 1 80341 838 4
978 1 78535 992 7 (ebook)
Library of Congress Control Number: 2025930189

A CIP catalogue record for this book is available from the British Library.

Design: Lapiz Digital Services

UK: Printed and bound by CPI Group (UK) Ltd, Croydon, CR0 4YY
US: Printed and bound by Thomson-Shore, 7300 West Joy Road, Dexter, MI 48130

Contents

This book is dedicated to my family, who kindly put up with the stress of living with an author. They've even been known to encourage me sometimes.

With thanks to Alex Murray for help with some modern Scottish folk beliefs and to Daniela Simina for assistance with Romanian material.

No generative AI was used in any way for any part of this book. All material was written by an actual person or quoted from the same.

Author's Note

Many of my books begin with questions that people ask me, however, this one is different. This book began, many years ago, as an article and then a series of conference papers aimed at answering a question no one was asking – what are the actual Scottish folk beliefs around the seelie and unseelie courts? For decades I had seen people in the US using the terms and had read about them in various novels, but it wasn't until the mid-2010s that I started to really question the wider popculture narrative around this subject. And once I started looking, I found that much of what is passed on both in popculture in the US and in paganism here is rooted not in actual Scottish folklore but in TV show plotlines and urban fantasy. I thought that it would be helpful not only to myself but to others to try to disentangle the roots of the fairy courts and show the various beliefs and their sources, so that others could also more easily navigate these confusing waters. I am a firm believer that the older, culturally specific beliefs have great value and that the world is poorer for their loss, something that is happening with increasing speed as the popculture narrative overwrites and erases the source material it is pulling from. Perhaps this book can, in some small way, slow that or at least offer a place for people to find the roots beneath the fictional tree that has sprung up.

I personally favour using APA citation in my writing and so throughout this book when a source is being cited you will see the name of the author and date of the book in parenthesis after that. This indicates the book that is being paraphrased in that sentence, both for clarity and to allow readers to further research for themselves if they choose to. I have also included endnotes expanding on points that don't fit neatly into the larger text but are important to touch on, as well as a selection of resources in Appendix B. This book will include portions of material from several previous university presentations I have given since 2019; these will be listed in the bibliography.

This book in no way seeks to judge what people believe or why, but hopefully it can help illuminate the wide range of ideas around the fairy courts and give people some sense of where these ideas are coming from. It wouldn't be possible to conduct an exhaustive survey of all of the modern beliefs or occurrences of these ideas across mass media, but I am including a range of material that I have found and which shows not only the variety of beliefs but also traces the development of many of these ideas across the last 50 years.

Introduction

"The Fairies, or Peaceable People, whom the Lowlanders call Seely Wights."

Jamieson, Popular Ballads and Songs

This text represents over a decade of focused research and incorporates material from several presentations I've given at University conferences. I find both the history of the fairy courts and their intersection with modern fiction fascinating, but it is also a subject about which there is a lot of confusion. This confusion comes, in part, from the blurring together of various sources and from misinformation that spreads from fiction into active belief, so this book is intended to help readers navigate the messiness of the subject by offering clear sources for various ideas and discussion of when and how different concepts merged or spread. I have also found that it can be very difficult, especially outside of academia, to find reliable information on the fairy courts, which may be why people are looking to fiction as a source instead.

Before we dive into all of that though we must start with a bit of semantics, to clarify the terms we're going to be using in this book and why they are being used that way. As we go through and explore both the history of the fairy courts as well as their modern iterations, I will be using the words fairy and elf interchangeably, which is how they are used in the older source material, but I acknowledge that given how the words are used today this can be confusing. In modern contexts the word fae has taken the place of fairy as a general catch-all term for Otherworldly beings and elf has come to be associated with beings that are more aligned with Tolkien's elves or those found across fantasy and urban fantasy novels. Historically, however, the two terms were often used synonymously for human-like magical beings and likely represented different cultural influences, with fairy coming from French while elf comes from Germanic sources. Professor Ronald Hutton, in a lecture on fairies in traditional English belief, suggested that the term fairy may have originally come in to replace the older Anglo-Saxon term elf (properly aelf) due to prohibitions around using a term that might offend these beings or attract their attention; interestingly this idea would later move to fairy which was avoided for similar reasons. In the border areas of Scotland which were influenced by Gaidhlig culture, English, and Germanic languages we find that fairy and elf are equated even into the early modern period, with sir Walter Scott, writing in the early 19th century, saying that the English fairy and Scottish elf were identical in how they were described and expected to act (Scott, 1831).

It may surprise some people to learn that there is some controversy around the use of the term fairy today, as the word is considered too imprecise and vague to be useful. Nonetheless it will be used in this text, as there is currently no ideal substitute. Throughout this book fairy will mean any of a variety of Otherworldly beings who may appear human, can shape shift, and have the ability to influence humans and the human world with magic.

Two other terms which need to be clarified now because they are such key concepts throughout this book are seelie and unseelie.[1] The words seelie and unseelie come to us from Scots, a language found on the Scottish borders which was influenced by Gaidhlig, English, and Norse languages. Seelie in Scots dictionaries is often associated with the fairies and given as an adjective to describe both a fairy court and the disposition of individual fairies themselves. Meanings for seelie are given ranging from happy, blessed, lucky, fortunate, and good natured, as well as having connotations of bringing good luck (DSL, 2016; Jamieson, 1808). In contrast unseelie means dangerous, unlucky, unfavourable, unhappy, unholy, and ungodly (DSL, 2016).

It should also be noted that the term unseelie referring to fairies is newer than the term seelie and does not appear in the Scots dictionary at all with this connotation, while seelie clearly does. The oldest reference to seelie for fairies is from a story dated to the late 1500's referenced in a book from 1801; this reference uses the term Seelie as a generic for fairy with no obvious distinction as to benevolence or malevolence, as do the other ballad references, supporting the idea that at some point there was likely only the concept of the single Seelie Court, used as a euphemism for all fairies. Much like the Welsh calling their fairies Tylwyth Teg [Fair Family] or the Irish use of the term Daoine Maithe [Good People] the Scottish Seelie Court, which can be understood as Blessed court or Happy court, may initially have been a way to speak of the fairies so that, should their attention be drawn, they would be more likely to be well disposed towards the speaker. This concept, at some later point was divided into seelie and unseelie to better define those beings who either meant humans well, generally, or meant humans harm, generally. The word unseelie can be found as far back as the 16th century meaning unlucky or miserable but has generally been applied to times, places, and animals; it was only applied to fairies much later (DSL, 2016).

Although much of this book will be discussing the Scottish Fairy Courts and their popculture offshoots we will also explore some other ways that western European fairies were understood. This includes the hierarchies found in Irish and English fairies. While it would be fair to just focus on the Scottish, I have found that too many people conflate the Scottish social structure out onto all fairies in a way that is both misleading and also erases other, older understandings found in specific cultures. Hopefully this book can help untangle all of that to show the ways these beings have been understood both within and outside the seelie/unseelie dynamic.

Chapter 1

Social Structure: Solitary, Trooping, and Courts

"'The night, the night is Halloween,
Our seely court maun ride,
Thro England and thro Ireland both,
And a' the warld wide."[2]

A fragment of Young Tamlane, Hinloch MSS, V, 391

In order to understand the concept of the fairy courts we need to start by taking a wider look at the main ways that fairies are socially understood. It has been a common trend since at least the late 19th century to view fairies and related beings as existing within two main social types: trooping and solitary. In this view the trooping fairies are the more social and communal of the fairies, while the solitary are, as one would assume, beings who exist outside social groupings. The trooping fairies can appear in a variety of sizes and forms and run the full range from helpful to humans, to dangerous to humans; they were often described wearing green (Briggs, 1976). In contrast the solitary fairies are more generally inclined towards harming humans and present a more blatant danger to them, although there are a few exceptions such as the Brownie who is known to help with housework and chores around the farm; the solitary fairies are more often described wearing red (Briggs, 1976). Green as a fairy colour is widely established across a range of material, so strongly associated with fairies that it was considered unlucky in some places for a Scottish woman to wear green and the ballad of *Alice Brand* refers to it as *'the fairies fatal green'*. Red is associated with these beings as well but almost always with the more dangerous kinds of beings and it can appear in stories as a visual or descriptive cue that the being in question is a threat.

It is the trooping fairies who would be associated with the courts over the last several hundred years, but this idea has changed in the 21st century due to the influence of urban fantasy – which we will discuss in depth in a later chapter – which has approached the idea of fairy courts not as a social grouping or by their approach to humans but as a moral alignment or as a default allegiance which all fairy beings must have. Starting in the early 19th century there would have been two social, or trooping, groups in Scottish folk belief with different connections to humans based on the risks they posed, as well as a third category of solitary fairies, however, as the solitary fairies were usually seen as more dangerous – usually predatory – towards humans they would eventually be lumped into the unseelie as well.

Although the rigid division of fairies into two courts is relatively modern and originally localized to the Scottish Lowlands, there is a more universal social structure that is followed in many areas with fairy beliefs: Monarchy. Although the details are not as fully fleshed out as a human monarchy we find references to various levels of society from low status servants to higher status ones, from knights and courtiers to nobles and rulers. The social structure here seems to have been a loosely feudal one, albeit a feudalism without the intrinsic land rights that define the human concept. Rather than the idea of a king or queen and nobles who own the land and are supported by tenant farmers we find that fairies' society was, in stories, based on pledges of fealty and service, through a hierarchical system with a king or queen at the top. In this version it is not land that is the baseline from which everything is worked but would seem to be scales of power. The weakest fairies – those with the least power – serve those with more, who in turn serve those with even more, on up to royalty, who are themselves often beings once understood or worshipped as Gods. This concept then leads us into the idea of courts, both the older understanding and the modern interpretations of it.

The next key concept to dig into then is the idea of courts.[3] It's important to understand that when we talk about fairy courts we may be talking about two distinctly different things. This double meaning and usage comes from the Scots language where the word court means both a group attending on royalty and more generally any group or company. Because much of our folklore about the courts in a general sense comes from the Scots speaking areas of Scotland this double usage of the word has found its way into modern fairylore, but a lack of understanding of the language means the nuance may be lost. For many today the idea of a court as any group has been lost in favour of the idea of the royal court, although that becomes cumbersome when expanded out to include all beings and so has come to be understood as if it were a political alignment. In older sources a group labelled, for example, seelie was simply one thought to be less dangerous to humans (unless motivated otherwise) but it wasn't immediately assumed they would all be loyal to one queen or king. In modern contexts, however, that has been lost so that there is or can be an assumption that anything labelled seelie would be aligned with a single monarch of the same affiliation.

So, firstly, the term fairy court is used as a general term to define an entire group of fairy beings, and by that understanding its nature is very broad. When we talk about the Seelie Court (or it's antithesis the Unseelie Court) we are not talking about a specific royal court, but are using the term in that second general sense for all types of beings who are either more or less immediately dangerous to humans. They may (or may not) owe allegiance to the monarchy of that court, the Queen of the Seelie Court or Nicnevin who is reputed to be Queen of the Unseelie, however, all beings with such allegiance are no more members of the royal court itself than all people in England are members of the English royal court. When we say they are part of the Seelie court we are using the term very generally, and that is probably the more common usage we find. The idea of this general use of 'Seelie court' started as a euphemism, a way to refer to all fairies in a positive manner which is why it is so intentionally inclusive.

The second way the word can be used, the first definition, relates to the specific group of beings who would attend or serve a Fairy Queen or King; we see this use in ballad material and in some anecdotes. In that case we are talking about a very specific grouping of individuals around and related to the Fairy royalty of a place. With this use of court, we swing from overly broad to very particular, which seems to be where the confusion comes in.

A royal court, fairy or human, is set up in roughly the same way and represents – effectively – the royal household. The royal court would include the ruling monarch, their immediate family, royal advisors and counsellors, courtiers,[4] court officials (such as the chancellor, purser, and chamberlain), entertainers, personal servants and some servants more generally, ladies-in-waiting, courtesans, knights, heralds, doorkeepers, cupbearers, ushers, grooms, huntsmen, and clergy (Pattie, 2011; C& MH, 2014). Ladies-in-waiting were usually the wives of nobles attending court (effectively courtiers) or sometimes widows of such nobles who had the task of keeping the Queen company, entertaining her, and keeping her up on the general goings-on at court as well as what was essential gossip; this could be an essential way for a monarch to stay aware of what was going on socially around them. The Queen would also have maidservants or handmaidens who were not nobility and were servants in truth that would handle her personal needs. Defining who was or wasn't in the court could be somewhat nebulous but effectively anyone who was in regular – usually daily or nearly daily – contact with the royal family and made their home at the royal court may be considered a member of the court. How many people a court was comprised of could vary widely from a relatively small number into the thousands depending on the size and power of a kingdom.

Being a member of the court did not mean having rank in it, however. Having rank within a court meant having a specific title and duty within that court relating to serving the monarch, and the system of rank as one may assume was hierarchical. Certain titles implied a great deal more power and influence than others, and some positions, like master huntsman or master falconer, where usually held by members of the nobility (C & MH, 2014). To quote the article 'Officers and Servants in a Medieval Castle': "*The presence of servants of noble birth imposed a social hierarchy on the household that went parallel to the hierarchy dictated by function*." (C & MH, 2014). This is referencing human royal courts; however, it applies equally to courts in Fairy; rank in a court is a matter equally of birth and function within the court itself, and everything is a matter of rank. This may be demonstrated in the ballad of *Tam Lin* where the eponymous character describes how the fairy court will ride out by sections based on rank:

> *"Then the first company which comes to you*
> *Is published king and queen;*
> *Then next the second company that comes to you,*
> *It is many maidens.*
> *Then next the company that comes to you*
> *Is footmen, grooms and squires;*
> *Then next the company that comes to you*
> *Is knights, and I'll be there."*
> Tan Lin 39G (modern English)

What we are seeing described is the fairy court riding out in procession in groups, with the royalty first, then the queen's ladies-in-waiting, then the more general retinue of servants, then the knights at the rear. This is fully in-line with what we might expect of a royal court, likely with other nobles riding along with the king and queen.

The court would be subdivided into sections by area of function and these in turn would be overseen by one individual and a series of lesser ranking assistants. Lower ranking members may wear the livery of the royal family to indicate specifically who they serve. Sections included the living quarters of the royals, the royal wardrobe, the stables, the kitchen, and hunting; each one was then subdivided sometimes into many smaller parts. The kitchen at large, for example, had a variety of very specific domains including: cooking area; buttery, pantry, confectionery, cellar, larder, spicery, saucery, scalding-house, and poultry (C & HM, 2014). A scullery maid would not likely interact with the Queen but would report to other lesser kitchen workers who in turn reported to higher ranking kitchen workers and on up the chain of command. Other sections were similarly complex, although how much or little would depend on the overall size of the household and court. If this sounds complicated that's because it is, and no less so for fairy courts than for human ones.

We should note that it is called a court for the same reason our modern legal court bears the name – because the royal court was a place where the Queen or King would make laws and give legal judgements. They would also receive tributes and taxes and generally take any actions to govern their country that was necessary. In this sense a royal court is both a collection of people and a place – it is the sum total of those people closest to the monarch but it is also the place that the monarch rules from. A portion of the officials at court would be people whose jobs would be assisting in overseeing the actual running of the country and implementation of the laws and orders of the monarch. This includes the exercise of military power as well as economic, which would be controlled by the monarch but delegated to court officials to actually handle executing. The location may be one set place, may move between several, or may always be changing. The court is, effectively, the centre of government for any monarchy.

The ruling monarch has a court; the members of their court do not have their own courts because only the ruling monarch has the authority to make governmental decisions, military decisions, and judgements of law. So, a Fairy Queen would have her court but her children and other close relatives would not have their own courts unless they are ruling monarchs in their own right of their own territory or have been given specific authority to rule as a representative of the Queen in a different location. In the same way, non-royal nobility do not generally have courts although in some rare cases they might depending on the degree of authority they have over their own territory. The monarch was, for all intents and purposes the heart of the royal court which existed around and for them.

When we see fairy courts portrayed in modern fiction they are often greatly simplified or not well explained which may give people a shallow view of what they are. A fairy court, whether that of the Seelie or Unseelie Queen or any of the Irish Fairy monarchs, would be complex and include a variety of beings that were part of the ruler's household, from close family to servants who waited on the royal family, as well as the same range listed above from advisors to huntsmen, although in the case of fairy courts there may be a greater emphasis on both knights and musicians or poets. These are usually beings who would be in permanent or near permanent attendance on the royal family, with the exception of knights who may be sent out or assigned specific tasks that took them away from the court. Again, we can look to Tam Lin as an example of this, as he was a knight within the Queen's court but had been given the task of guarding a specific well in the forest of Carterhaugh. Courtiers, especially nobles, may also spend part of their time away from court, but would generally be expected to spend most of their time attending to the Queen or King.

To understand and appreciate the fairy courts we need an understanding of what they are. Human royalty still exists in some places and still have courts, although largely symbolic now, and there is no indication that fairies do not still operate with a monarchy system which would include royal courts. At the least understand that these courts would include the royal household as well as courtiers, and that rank within a court would be an intersecting matter of birth and function. Everyone in a court has a function which ultimately serves the monarch, and the court itself is both representative of the monarch's power and a tool to exercise that power.

When we discuss the subjects of fairies' social structure it is helpful to keep all of this in mind, the ideas of trooping vs solitary, the dual meanings of court, and the wider idea of what a royal court is. These concepts tend to weave together to create the full picture of the fairy court across folk belief.

Chapter 2
Scottish Fairy Beliefs

"Ane Carling of the Quene of Phareis
that ewill win gair to elphyne careis;
Through all Braid Albane scho hes bene
On horsbak on Hallow ewin;
and ay in seiking certayne nyghtis
As scho sayis, with sur sillie wychtis"[5]

Legend of the Bishop of St Androis

Before we jump fully into discussing the courts we must, perforce, lay some groundwork about the Scottish fairy beliefs which form the foundation of the ideas around the courts. Although later in this book we will explore ways that the idea of the courts has become embedded in popculture, especially urban fantasy, it is impossible to understand these concepts without looking to their source, and equally impossible to truly understand that source without at least a basic understanding of the wider early modern Scottish beliefs around fairies.

As with such beliefs anywhere else the Scottish fairy beliefs are not a cohesive whole but a collection of various regional folk beliefs, which were each influenced by the cultures they interacted with. This means that the Gaidhlig speaking areas have slightly different ideas about fairies compared to the border areas, and that we may find a concept attributed in one place to fairies and in another to witches. While the next chapter will be exploring concepts that originated in the southern border areas, this chapter will have a slightly wider focus, to offer a fuller view of fairy beliefs across Scotland from the early modern period onwards.

As mentioned previously, in Scotland we find the terms elf and fairy used interchangeably in English speaking material. In Gaidhlig these beings are 'am Daoine Sìth', the people of the sìth; the word sìth can mean fairy hill, fairy, or peace and sometimes Daoine sìth is given as people of peace. A variety of other euphemisms are used for these beings as well including Silently Moving People, Still People, Sleagh Maith [Good People], and the Good Neighbours (Kirk, 2007; Campbell, 1900; Henderson, 1997). Both Rev. Kirk writing in the 17th century and John Gregerson Campbell writing in the late 19th century described the Scottish fairies as intrinsically connected to humanity, beings who mimicked or mirrored human life but existed apart from it, who engaged in common human activities like weaving, cooking, and hunting but who lived within the earth or beneath it; Kirk labelled them 'Subterraneans' because of this. It is clear, however, in folk stories that the fairies were not thought to live underground in the sense that a human might dig out a home in the earth but rather that they lived in another realm contained beneath the ground. This has led to a common and widespread conflation of the Scottish fairies and the human dead or ancestors, a belief which is stronger and clearer in Scotland than in other Celtic language speaking cultures. It is simultaneously true that some folklore and ballad material indicates the fairies live in a distinct and separate world which is not necessarily beneath the ground. This idea is illustrated in the ballad of *Thomas the Rhymer* where Thomas journeys into Elfland with the Fairy Queen by traversing various terrain not by going underground.

In almost all ways the fairies of Scotland are similar to humans, except with a greater magical ability. They may look much like a human being and often act, or try to act, human, yet are able to command magical powers and may do things that seem inexplicable or cruel. They were also renowned for their wisdom, ability to see the future, and craftsmanship which excelled human equivalents. Sir Walter Scott, writing in 1831, said of elves:

> *"Their attributes, amongst which we recognize the features of the modern Fairy, were supernatural wisdom and prescience, and skill in the mechanical arts, especially in the fabrication of arms. They are further described as capricious, vindictive, and easily irritated."* (Scott, 1931, p288).

Scottish fairies also held a place that was uniquely close to the demonic, compared to other post-Christian western European cultures which might describe fairies as a type of fallen angel but usually placed them either within their own category of being or viewed them as belonging to the limbo of purgatory as fallen angels who were not bad enough for Hell. Belief in fairies persisted across the centuries in Scotland, but faced a cosmological conundrum, in that the Christian worldview allowed for only two classes of spirit, beyond humans: angels and demons. Fairies with their penchant for mercurialness and harming as frequently as blessing hardly seemed to qualify as angels which left only the realm of the demonic open to them in the stricter Scottish Protestant views. As sir Walter Scott put it: *"The fairies were, therefore…regarded as actual demons, or something very little better."* (Scott, 1931, p 307). This was in line with wider contemporary ecclesiastical Scottish belief, which contrasted the goodness and rightness of Christianity against the supernatural which was categorized as demonic in nature (Walsh, 2002). While earlier folk belief may have taken a more lenient view of fairies and understood them as neutral or ambivalent beings, the early modern period saw a change in this as the religious view of fairies moved them more firmly into the realm of the Devil (Henderson& Cowan, 2007). The fairies remained a fixture of folk belief, and remained within a more neutral third class of spirits in that belief, but this view was rejected by the churches of the time which instead taught that fairies were equivalent to demons.

It was common from the 16th through 18th centuries for fairies or elves to be equated to imps as well as succubi or incubi, reinforcing the wider idea that they were a class of demon, if of a slightly less evil nature, and showing the tension between church and folk belief. The *Flyting Betwixt Montgomerie and Polwart* provides a very early 17th century example of this, and of the wider crossover between terms: *"The King of Pharie and his court, with the Elfe Queene; With many Elrich Jncubus was rydand that Night"*[6] (Hume, 1629). In this we see fairies and elves intermixed and 'elvish' used as an adjective describing incubi. The late 17th century witchcraft indictment against Jean Weir stated that she was hired by a woman to speak *"to the Queen of Fairii, meaning the devil"*, with the text making clear that no distinction was seen between the two by the ecclesiastical audience (Scott, 1931). The embedded cultural crossover between fairies and demons may also be illustrated by an 1820's variant of the ballad *The Elfin Knight* recorded by Andrew Crawford under the title *The Deil's Wouing* which substitutes the Devil for the otherwise eponymous Elf.

Reverend Kirk explained the fairies' aversion to iron in relation to their connection to demons and to Hell, saying that:

> *"...all uncouth, unknown Wights are terrified by nothing earthly so much as by cold Iron. They deliver the Reason to be that Hell lying betwixt the chill Tempests, and the Fire Brands of scalding Metals, and Iron of the North... by an Antipathy thereto, these odious far-scenting Creatures shrug and fright at all that comes thence relating to so abhorred a Place, whence their Torment is either begun, or feared to come hereafter"* (Kirk & Warner, 2007, pp 11-12).

By this reasoning the fairies flee from iron because it reminds them of the fate that awaits them in Hell, just as they flee at

Christian invocations which remind them of the salvation they are denied.

Despite this overt association with the Devil and demons across folk belief in the early modern period fairies themselves were not seen as inherently evil or always dangerous, especially to those who treated them with respect. Although the relationship between some witches and fairies is complex, we can say that many early modern Scottish witches benefited from the generosity of the fairies, with Isobel Gowdie talking about being given meat (a luxury food for her), Bessie Dunlop saying she was offered 'goods and gear' by the fairy Queen and Andro Mann being taught healing and magical skills that allowed him to practice as a cunningman. Similarly in the ballad of *Alison Gross* the Fairy Queen removes the protagonist's curse for no discernible reason beyond kindness. The risk they presented was a potential one, not an inevitable one.

That said, while fairies could be helpful and blessing to those they liked, or even in same cases randomly, they could also be quite vicious especially against those who wronged them. A rhyme found in an 1819 Edinburgh magazine illustrates this in describing the consequences of disturbing a fairy green or ring:

"He wha tills the fairy green
Nae luck again sall hae
An' he wa spills the fairy ring
Betide him want and wae
For weirdless days and weary nichts
Are his til his deean day"[7]
(On Good and Bad Fairies, 1819)

Fairies who had been angered or were malicious might employ a particular weapon known as elf shot or elf arrows – saighead sìth in Gaidhlig – which caused sudden symptoms including paralysis, seizure, cramping, or bruising and were associated with both wasting sicknesses and death; elf shot's most common result was a sharp, unexplained, shooting internal pain (Briggs, 1976; Hall, 2007). The symptoms of elfshot were called the elf stroke or fairy stroke, a term that may be related to the modern term stroke for a cerebral haemorrhage or accident. If the fairies were punishing someone for a minor offence or annoyance the symptoms might be slight or temporary, while if they intended to torment the person the effects would be permanent and severe. Similarly, if they wanted to steal a human or animal, they might use elfshot to paralyze them before switching the human for a changeling (Briggs, 1976). In several witch trials accused witches confessed to using elfshot to harm others, and Isobel Gowdie in her confession claimed to have seen the shot being made when she was visiting among the fairies (Briggs, 1976). In her telling she said she had gone with the fairies and saw the Devil himself making the shot and handing it to 'elf boys' who sharpened them and prepared them. She claimed that they were then given to the mortal witches to be used with a short chant and that the shot was fired by being flicked off the thumb with a fingernail (Black, 1894; Briggs, 1976).

The Sìthe and the Dead

There is a pervasive and complex overlap between fairies and the human dead, particularly ancestors, in Scotland. While the church was strong in its condemnation of fairies as demons the laity was less swayed by this view and might have a different view of these beings which placed them, at least tangentially, among the human dead in some way. The idea that the dead can be or represent part of the fairy host is an old one and in more modern Scottish fairylore has become stronger. Across the years it's been suggested that fairies were the pagan dead, ghosts, or even the preserved memory of an earlier group of humans who had been driven out of the area (Henderson & Cowan, 2007). Although this view wasn't universal and other opinions also existed, including that the fairies were spirits of the natural world, demons, angels, or demoted pagan gods, this connection between the two groups, fairies and human dead, is nonetheless pervasive and lingering and is especially strong in Scottish belief. Several accused witches in the 17th century claimed that they associated with fairies and had been given a familiar spirit from among the fairies who had originally been human (Henderson & Cowan, 2007; Wilby, 2005). In the ballad of *Alice Brand,* the Fairy King sets one of his people on two interlopers to his forest and it is eventually revealed that the fairy who was sent was once a human man who fell in battle and was taken by the fairies.

Scott Richardson-Read ties fairy belief to animism and connects the idea of the Gods – themselves also deeply tied to the fairies – to the ancestral dead. He also suggests both through the etymology of the word sìth and the common association of the sìth with burial mounds that there could have been an assumed tie between these spirits and ancestors. This idea if reinforced in Henderson and Cowans' book *Scottish Fairy Belief* where the authors note that many of the places associated with fairies and where offerings to them might be left were neolithic burial mounds.

The subject is more complex than a simple one-to-one equivalency, and in other contexts and stories fairy beings are described as existing outside humanity but as with the association with demons this aspect of belief is important to understand. Fairy belief is layered and nuanced in ways that offer suggestions rather than firm answers.

The Sluagh Sìth

Related to the concept of fairies and the dead in Scottish belief we find a particular group of fairies, the Sluagh Sìth, who are considered both fairies and, in some stories, human spirits. Sluagh Sìth is a Gaidhlig term meaning Fairy People or Fairy

Host and may be shortened to Sluagh, while Sluagh na Sìthe is a poetic term for the fairies. In Scottish folklore the Sluagh may be understood as fairies but are also described as being the unforgiven human dead who kill animals and restlessly wander the skies (McNeill, 1956; Briggs, 1976; Carmichael, 1900). It is believed that they lived wicked lives as humans and must therefore atone for their sins by wandering the earth without rest. They may employ elfshot, invisible arrows, against their victims and by some accounts serve or are driven by another spirit; Alexander Carmichael in his *Carmina Gadelica* doesn't name or describe these beings, only referring to them as 'spirit-masters'.

Irish folklore has a different term, slua na marbh, for the host of the dead, however, Gaidhlig doesn't differentiate the two in the same way. This illustrates the blurred lines in Scottish belief between the fairies and the dead.

The Sìth and Changelings

Across all Celtic language speaking cultures the fairies are known to steal humans, although the reason for this may vary. In the ballad *The Queen of Elfin's Nourice*[8] a human woman is taken just after giving birth for the purpose of wet-nursing the Fairy Queen's infant son. In the ballad of *Thomas the Rhymer* the Fairy Queen takes Thomas to be her lover while in *Tam Lin* the stolen human is set to guard a well that belongs to the fairies. In various folkloric accounts humans were taken for those reasons, as well as to provide additional numbers to the fairy host – human women providing children to the fairies and human children taken to be raised among them. The fairies have the ability to change a human into a fairy, something that is discussed in some versions of *Tam Lin* where Tam, stolen as a child, tells his human lover what it is like to be a fairy and mentions things like changing size which would be impossible for a human to do. Another possible reason for a human to be taken by the fairies is to pay the fairies' tithe, which will be discussed in depth below. Although some humans are turned into fairies and trapped forever (usually) among them, some others are only taken temporarily; this would usually include musicians or midwives who are borrowed to serve a specific purpose and wouldn't fall under the label of changeling. Fairies may also steal humans in order to torment them for the fairies' own entertainment.

When a human is taken permanently a changeling could be left in their place. A changeling may be an inanimate object, an old fairy looking to be cared for, or a sickly fairy infant which would be exchanged for a healthy human one; all would be disguised magically as the stolen human. In most cases the changeling would sicken and die, leaving the humans to mourn the person they thought had passed without knowing that they had actually been taken by the fairies. In some cases, usually where an old fairy was involved, the human family would become suspicious, consult a specialist, and find a way to get the fairy to reveal itself. This usually involved either catching the fairy engaging in a skilled task, like playing an instrument, or in tricking it into speaking openly in front of its new 'family'; the most well-known example of this is a mother boiling water in an eggshell causing the fairy to exclaim that in a thousand years he'd never seen such a thing. Once revealed the fairy must leave and the human is automatically returned. In a few other stories the stolen human might be rescued from the fairies using a process through which they are won away from them – the ballad of *Tam Lin* is an extreme illustration of this where Tam is saved from the fairies when his human lover withstands a test of courage by holding onto him as the Fairy Queen transforms him into various terrifying things. Most other methods of rescuing a changeling involved violent treatment of the suspected changeling, with the idea that this would force the fairies to take it back and in so doing to return the human who had been taken. The deaths of children and adults have resulted from this.

The Tithe to Hell[9]

One concept which is unique to the border beliefs, specifically near Selkirk and Melrose on the banks of the Tweed, is that these beings owe a regular payment to Hell; this in turn was embedded in the idea that the Good Neighbours were a kind of 'demon lite', beings who were numbered among the denizens of Hell but were not evil enough to be truly demonic. The idea of the fairies' rent paid to Hell was originally localized around the river Tweed in Scotland, and has only recently gained wider recognition, but it provides important insight into the way that fairies were conceptualized during this period.

The fairies' tithe to hell is an idea which says that fairies must make a payment to Hell in the form of souls on a set schedule, most often said to be every seven years (Briggs, 1976). The exact terms, however, vary between different sources: the written sources and ballads claim it is due every seven years, while the single account of the tithe from the witchcraft trials places it as a yearly payment. It is also called both a tithe and a kane depending on the source; a tithe is a payment of a tenth part, in this case implied to be a tenth of the fairy population, while kane is a Scots word for a rental payment to a landlord (Lyle, 1970). The key difference between the two here would be in the number of souls paid, as a tithe implies many while a kane could be significantly less. Indeed, the various texts of *Tam Lin* often have him say of the imminent tithe '*I fear 'twill be myself*' suggesting that he expects to be the only one given to Hell (Lyle, 1970). In at least one variant version found in Campbell's collection when Tam Lin is safely won away from the fairies by his human lover, the Fairy Queen declares that, having lost him, she believes that she herself will be used to pay the kane (Wimberly, 1965).

The textual evidence for the tithe is initially found in the 15th century text *Thomas of Erceldoune,* later known in ballad form as *Thomas the Rhymer* and is tied to the area around Dryburgh Abbey and Melrose along the river Tweed (Murray, 1918). The second oldest literary source for the tithe comes from *The Ballad of Tam Lin* dating to the 16th century set at Carterhaugh in Selkirk, located along one of the tributaries of the Tweed (Murray, 1872). The two locations are about eight miles apart, however, the next reference to the tithe comes from the late 16th century witchcraft trial of a woman named Alison Pearson, from Fife about 80 miles north, perhaps showing how the belief was spreading across the years.

Thomas of Erceldoune references the Devil fetching his fee from the fairies and suggests that Thomas will be chosen because he is so strong and pleasant:

"To Morne, of helle the foulle fende,
Amange this folke will feche his fee;
And thou arte mekill mane and hende,
I trowe wele he wode chese thee."[10]
(Murray, 1918)

In the same way Tam Lin says that:

"But aye at every seven years,
They pay the teind to Hell;
And I am sae fat and fair of flesh
I fear 'twill be mysell.'
(Child, 1886)

Alison Pearson claimed to have learned her skill as a cunningwoman from the fairies and in her trial testimony said *"every year the tithe of [the fairies] were taken away to Hell"* and that her guide among the fairies, a deceased uncle, had urged her to bless and sain herself and avoid going with the fairies again in order not to be given as part of this tithe (Scott, 1830; Wilby, 2009). Based on all of this the belief may have varied in how often the payment was made and its nature, but establishes that the fairies were required to pay Hell on a regular basis, and that this payment was often understood as a rent payment.

The core concept behind the fairies' payment was the idea that as a lesser kind of demon they were under the purview of the Devil and his domain and so owed him rent on a set basis. In this context the land of Fairy became a kind of sublet area of Hell, which belonged properly to the Devil but was in use by the fairies. Their rent is paid in the stereotypical currency of Hell – souls. Lyle's article *The Teind to Hell in Tam Lin* argues that the belief in the teind grew out of a need to explain the belief in changelings, those objects or dying fairies left in exchange for healthy humans, often babies or children (Lyle, 1970). From this perspective in seeking to understand why fairies stole human beings people came to fit them into the demonic view put forth by the church of the time, that fairies were lesser demons who lived as tenants to the Devil, they were required to pay rent to the Devil for the land of Fairy, and did so by stealing humans to spare having to give up their own folk. A key aspect to this argument is the fact that in both poems the teind is due to be paid the next morning and the men in the story can be saved that night if they escape Fairyland before the payment (Lyle, 1970). In *Tam Lin* this occurs exactly on Samhain, modern Halloween, a time in Scotland when the bi-annual rents came due, reinforcing the idea that the tithe or kane was explicitly a rent payment (Lyle, 1970).

The Question of Morality

One final subject which must be touched on here is morality of fairies, as it is understood, because as we delve into the idea of the seelie and unseelie there are some assumptions that tend to be made based on human morality which is a foreign system to the fairy folk. It is well established across folklore that fairies are, despite an often-human appearance, foreign beings from a foreign culture. Katherine Briggs may explain the role of fairies in relation to human morals best, saying *'(t)he fairies, as one would expect, have no special bias towards respectability...'* (Briggs, 1967). In places and cultures where humans are not allowed to dance or must do so within a rigid structure, fairies are known to dance wildly and without restraint. Where humans are encouraged to focus on work and accomplishing tasks, we find stories of fairies engaged in leisurely activities including riding and dancing (Wimberly, 1965). Where humans are expected to be chaste and reserved, fairies are sexually open and promiscuous. This shows not only the way that fairies often contradict human behavioural expectations but also that the very nature of fairies was understood to be different from humanity. They bless and curse on their own whim and following their own standards, rewarding those they like with blessings and harshly punishing those who offend them or commit even the smallest breach of fairy etiquette. Fairy reactions in situations may not match expected human ones, they may seem too minimal or too extreme, and fairies are often described as cruel. Through this lens then we must try to understand fairies not as morally good or bad, by human standards, but as beings who exist outside human morality.

This is by no means an exhaustive look at Scottish fairies, but hopefully has given readers a basic understanding of them. Henderson and Cowan's book *Scottish Fairy Belief* is a good resource to learn more, although it primarily focuses on the early modern period. Several of the key points in this chapter are important foundational elements to the next chapter and to a wider understanding of the Scottish Fairy Courts, and even later popular culture understandings of both fairies/elves and the courts which are all ultimately rooted in the Scottish material.

Chapter 3
The Scottish Fairy Courts

"But as it fell out on last Halloween
When the seely court was riding by
The queen lighted down on a rowan bank
Not far frae the tree where I wont to lie."
The Ballad of Allison Gross

The practice of dividing Fairy into courts is one that many people may be familiar with, and which people often seem to assume is quite old. The reality is more complex and begins in the Lowlands of Scotland with the Seelie court and later the complimentary Unseelie court; these ideas became ingrained in Scottish folklore and, now, in wider culture. References to the Seelie court first appear 500 years ago, and the Unseelie court within the last 200 years or so, originally regionally specific. As with many fairy beliefs an idea becomes popular and then enters the mainstream in some sense, often carried on the currents of contemporary popular culture, and once adopted is accepted into the corpus of fairy belief. The seelie and unseelie are often simplified as the 'good' and 'bad' fairies, or as F. Marian McNeill says the *'gude wichts'*[11] *and the 'wicked wichts'* based in how each group is most likely to interact with humans (McNeill, 1956). Evidence for this can easily be seen by looking at the sources we have available to us: references to the Seelie court are focused in the border and lowland areas, while authors writing elsewhere – from Rev. Robert Kirk[12] in the 17th century to John Campbell in the 19th – make no mention of the term despite writing in great detail on folk beliefs around Scottish fairies. I think we lose the nuances between the two when we try to reduce them into such blunt terms as good and bad (or worse good and evil) and also that many modern people may not fully understand the concepts of seelie and unseelie.

The words seelie and unseelie come to us from Scots, itself an amalgam of a variety of languages found in the Lowland areas of Scotland. Although its most often seen today as 'Seelie' it also appears in older texts in a variety of forms including seely, seily, sealy, with seely being the most common (DSL, 2016). It is often a term in Scots dictionaries associated with the fairies and given as an adjective to describe both a fairy court and the disposition of individual fairies themselves. Meanings for seelie are given ranging from happy, blessed, lucky, fortunate, and good natured, as well as having connotations of bringing good luck (DSL, 2016; Jamieson, 1808). In contrast unseelie – also spelled oonseely, onseely, unsealy, or unseely – means dangerous, unlucky, unfavourable, unhappy, unholy, and ungodly (DSL, 2016). The word unseelie, in the form of unsely, can be found as far back as the 16th century meaning unlucky or miserable but has generally been applied to times, places, and animals (DSL, 2016). I have been unable to find any references to unseelie being applied to fairies prior to the 19th century.

The Seelie court is described in relation to the fairies specifically as the "*pleasant or happy court, or court of the pleasant and happy people*" and is also given as a general term for all fairies (Jamieson, 1808). In folklore the Seelie court can act benevolently at times for no reason other the sake of kindness, as we see in the 1783 ballad '*Allison Gross*', where the eponymous witch of the story punishes a man who refused her sexual advances by bespelling him into the shape of a worm. The unfortunate man is cursed to circle around a tree every day in this form, until one Halloween "*when the seely court was riding by*" and the queen stops, picks up the worm, and uses her magic to restore his original shape to him (Child, 1886). They are also known to be extremely generous to those whom they favour and to be kind to the poor, giving bread and grain as gifts (Briggs, 1976). It was believed that members of the Seelie court would help those who propitiated them and that this help took various forms including the fairy doing work for the human around their home or farm (McNeill, 1956). Despite its reputation as generally kindly, the Seelie court was known to readily revenge any wrongs or slights against themselves, and even a fairy who would be considered Seelie could be dangerous when offended or harmed. The Seelie court is not known to harm people without reason though and generally will warn people at least once before retaliating against offenses (Briggs, 1976).

The Seelie court can also act in ways that go against what we would consider goodness, or at least in ways that bring harm to humans, without a clear reason. We see this in the *Ballad of Lady Mary O' Craignethan* where the Lord's daughter is quite deviously kidnapped by a man of the sìth to be his bride; the Lord then curses the fairy folk, wishing that the Devil may take three of them instead of one as his tithe, and swearing to cut down every oak, beech, and ash in the country to which the priest begs him *"dinnae curse the Seelie Court"* (Sand, Brymer, Murray, & Cochran, 1819). This illustrates that it was in fact the Seelie court that was believed to be behind the kidnapping, although as we shall see later, the term Seelie court itself may have served as a euphemism for all fairies, rather than a specific term only for the benevolent ones.

The Unseelie court is for all intents and purposes the antithesis of the Seelie court, as implied by the name. The Unseelie court is described as always unfavourable to humans and is closely linked to the Sluagh sìth, the malicious Host who torment people and cause illness and death where they visit (Briggs, 1976). The Sluagh itself is strongly tied to the dead and is known to kidnap hapless mortals and force them to help with the Host's entertainment, usually harming other humans, before dropping them in a location far from where they were grabbed. The Unseelie court is comprised of many solitary fairies of a malicious nature, those who feed on or enjoy hurting mortals for sport, although not all Unseelie fairies are solitary (Briggs, 1976). The Unseelie court was seen as constantly ready to cause harm or injury to mortals and were avoided as much as possible, and many different protections existed against them (McNeill, 1956; Briggs, 1976).

However, just as the Seelie court could cause harm if motivated to, and sometimes without having any clear reason at all, so too the Unseelie court's denizens may occasionally act kindly towards humans without any obvious rhyme or reason. For example, Kelpies are usually considered Unseelie by most reckonings, as they trick people into riding them only to kill and eat the person once they have gotten back to their watery homes, however, in several stories a Kelpie will fall in love with a mortal girl and put aside his own bloodthirsty nature for her sake. In one such story the Kelpie even put up with being tricked by the girl, captured himself and forced to work in his horse form on her father's farm for a year, and still loved her enough in the end to choose to marry her (McNeill, 2001). So, while it may be convenient and often expedient to divide the fairies up into the two courts based on how they relate to us, we should be very cautious about seeing the division as a hard line or seeing a perceived placement in one court or another as a non-negotiable indicator of behaviour.

As mentioned above the term seelie may not have been as specific in the past as it is today and when we look at its usage in older ballads and stories seelie often appears as a euphemism (DSL, 2016). That means that just like calling Themselves 'Good Neighbours', 'Mother's Blessing', or 'Fair Folk' it isn't done because they are those things but because we want them to be those things towards us. In other words, we are using a euphemism – a nicer term for something generally considered not nice at all – to try to invoke the nicer aspects of them. To remind them that they can be nice. There is long standing and deep belief that what we choose to call the Fey directly relates to how they will respond to us and interact with us. As this 1842 rhyme illustrates:

"Gin ye ca' me imp or elf
I rede ye look weel to yourself;
Gin ye call me fairy
I'll work ye muckle tarrie;
Gind guid neibour ye ca' me
Then guid neibour I will be;
But gin ye ca' me seelie wicht
I'll be your freend baith day and nicht."[13]
(Chambers, 1842)

It should also be noted that the term unseelie referring to fairies is newer than the term seelie and does not appear in the Scots dictionary at all with this connotation, while seelie clearly does. The oldest reference I could find to seelie for fairies is from a story dated to the 1500's referenced in a book from 1801; in the *Legend of the Bishop of St Androis* it says:

"Ane Carling of the Quene of Phareis
that ewill win gair to elphyne careis;
Through all Braid Albane scho hes bene
On horsbak on Hallow ewin;
and ay in seiking certayne nyghtis
As scho sayis, with sur sillie wychtis"[14]

This reference uses the term Seelie as a generic for fairy with no obvious distinction as to benevolence or malevolence, as do the other ballad references, supporting the idea that at some point there was likely only the concept of the single Seelie Court, used as a euphemism for all fairies. We see much the same in a 1564 lecture by William Hays discussing woman labelled witches who dealt with fairies where he refers to *'celly vychtis'* [seelie wichts] and in a 1572 witchcraft trial account where a woman talks of an infant stolen by the 'sillyie wichts'. In both examples seelie wicht is being used as a general term for fairies, almost certainly in a euphemistic sense, especially in the second case where they were not acting at all benevolently. Much like the Welsh calling their fairies Tylwyth Teg [Fair Family] or the Irish use of the term Daoine Maithe [Good People] the Scottish Seelie Court [Blessed court or Happy court] may initially have been a way to speak of the fairies so that should their attention be drawn, they would be more likely to be well disposed towards the speaker. This concept, at some later point was divided into seelie and unseelie to better define those beings who either meant humans well, generally, or meant humans harm, generally. While it may seem strange to us now, it is entirely logical that in the past people would have used the euphemistic Seelie Court when referring to the fairies, but not had an inverse negative concept as it would have been seen as impossibly dangerous to even speak of such a group and risk drawing their attention and facing their wrath for it. This could also explain why the idea of the courts as such is unique to Lowland Scots lore and more generally Scottish folklore. It is not found in Welsh or Irish fairylore[15] where different euphemisms are used and where there is no concept of dividing the fairies by 'good' or 'bad'.

The earliest reference I have found to the Unseelie as a distinct grouping of fairies is in an 1819 article titled *On Good and Bad Fairies* in The Edinburgh Magazine and Literary Miscellany. The article begins by explaining that fairies exist within two groups: the good fairies or seelie court and the wicked fairies or unseelie court. While arguing that both groups are supplemented by humans who have been denied a Christian afterlife, it argues that the seelie court take humans who are basically good, drawing from the ranks of abused infants, the righteous battle dead, and those who complained about their difficult lives, citing the ballad of Sir Orfeo's description of the humans within the Fairy King's court as evidence. In contrast it claims the Unseelie court is peopled by those who fell in unrighteous battles, who made pacts with unholy forces, or were unwed mothers who died in childbirth[16] and unbaptized babies, adding that it was only this court who paid the teind to Hell with the implication that they deserved such a fate (an idea not found elsewhere). According to the article any parent who spoke ill of their own child or wished them harm might find the child stolen by the fairies, with baptized children going to the seelie court and unbaptized ones taken by the unseelie. Much emphasis is put on Christian salvation throughout the text, with the author suggesting that the seelie, because of their inherent goodness, might still attain Heaven while the unseelie were lost to Hell, excepting only those fortunate souls who might be won back from the fairies by a living human.

It is worth noting again that while we are referring to these groupings as the Scottish Fairy Courts these beliefs were not in fact common in all areas of Scotland. As the terms themselves come from Scots, which is a language found in the lowland and border areas, it shouldn't be a surprise that in areas which retained more Gaidhlig speakers, particularly in the north west, the fairies were understood slightly differently with the wider grouping seen as ambivalent and mercurial and the more dangerous spirits, usually associated with water, called the Fuath. With the definitive article, am Fuath, the term is translated as 'the fairies' but without that the word itself means aversion, hatred, spectre (Dwelly, 1967).

In any part of Scottish belief, the fairies are thought to exist in a social structure similar to their human neighbours which includes royalty, or as Reverend Kirk put it in the late 17th century: *"They are said to have aristocraticall Rulers and Laws"* (Kirk & Lang, 1893, p 15). 100 years prior to Kirk's writing King James

VI[17] offered more detail in his *'Daemonologie'* when he related the local Catholic beliefs about fairies: *"[T]here was a King and Queene of Phairie of such a jolly court & train as they had, how they had a teynd, & dutie, as it were, of all goods: how they naturallie rode and went, eate and drank, and did all other actiones like naturall men and women."*[18] (James I, 1924, p 74). Although James VI spoke of a King and Queen of Fairy in this passage most of his writing on fairies focused only on a Fairy Queen, who he positioned as both an important figure in belief as well as a being who people claimed to interact directly with, including those accused of witchcraft who claimed to have been granted power or abilities through the fairies, including accounts where a person claimed to have been given a magical stone by the Fairy Queen.

If we understand the Seelie and Unseelie courts, by either definition of the term court, to be monarchies then it then begs the question who would rule these groups? It may surprise some people to learn that while the idea of a Fairy King is relatively common today in older belief the emphasis tended to be on Fairy Queens, as we find, for example, in King James VI's writing. This may have represented an inversion of the power structures of the human world reflected in giving the greatest power to a female ruler rather than the male ruler common in the related human cultures. Due to this most of the references we have to rulers of the Scottish Fairy Courts focus on the queen or on a king paired with a queen.

In most sources the Fairy Queen or King are not named, but only referred to by title. We see this across the ballad material, from the *Queen of Elfin's Nourice* to *Tam Lin,* as well as prose material like *Thomas of Erceldoune,* where the Queen is described and may feature prominently as a character but is never named, nor is her king in examples where he is also mentioned. In *The Tale of Alice Brand,* for example, the Elf King is not named and his queen is only mentioned in passing, also without a name. Scottish witch Isobel Gowdie described the fairy king as a handsome man but never named him, and similarly the queen of fairy was described in many accounts as beautiful, clad in green or white velvet, but never given a name. Kruse in his book *How Things Work In Faery* suggests one possible explanation for this avoidance was that *"Faery royalty are so exalted that none may speak their names"* or alternately that the exact opposite held true and the Fairy Queen was so prosaic and ordinary in her nature and activities that her role was rendered rather anonymous (Kruse, 2021, p 29). These seemingly antithetical possibilities nicely encapsulate the nature of Fairy, which is always contradictory and difficult to entirely sort out. There are, however, a few instances where names are given, which will be discussed, or the Queen is linked to a specific court which serves as a kind of stand in name.

Seelie Queen – Most of the time when a queen of the fairies or elves is mentioned she is not named or may be referred to simply as the 'Seelie Queen'. This term in older sources (before the 1800s) is effectively interchangeable with Elf Queen or Fairy Queen as a general name for the ruler of the Good Folk. The Seelie Queen usually appears alone, but may sometimes be seen with an unnamed King or riding with a retinue if knights. She is often described as peerlessly beautiful, dressed in green, and riding on a white horse. In the ballad of *Thomas the Rhymer* Thomas initially confuses her for the Virgin Mary until she corrects him.

The Seelie Queen can be both benevolent and cruel, depending on her mood. In the ballad of *Alison Gross* she comes across a man who has been turned into a worm by a witch's curse and frees him, for no clear reason beyond kindness. In contrast the Fairy Queen in the ballad of *Tam Lin,* identified in some versions as the Seelie Queen, steals a young Tam away from his human family to keep for herself, is willing to give him up to the fairies' tithe to Hell, and when Tam is successfully freed by his human lover she both threatens to curse the woman and says that she should have either turned his heart to stone or taken his eyes out to prevent him falling in love with her. In *The Faerie Oak of Corriewater* the Fairy Queen steals a young man away from his family and when his sister tries to rescue him, she tests her with magic, resulting in the girl's death by fire.

Nicnevin – the main female figure named in connection to the Scottish Fairy Courts is Nicnevin, an obscure but fascinating figure from northern Scottish folk belief. She first appears in writing in a 16th century poem by Alexander Montgomerie, '*The Flyting Betwixt Montgomerie and Polwart*', which says:

"Nicneuen with hir Nymphis, in nomber anew,
With charmes from Caitness and Chanrie in Rosse,
Quhais cunning consistis in casting a clew...
The King of pharie, and his Court, with the elph queine,
With mony elrich Incubus was rydand that nycht."[19]

From this people extrapolate that Nicnevin is the Queen of these beings and connect her to the 'Elf Queen' also referenced in the poem. Her king is unnamed both in the poem and elsewhere. In more recent folk belief Nicnevin is understood as the Queen of the Unseelie court specifically. Likely based on Sir Walter Scott's description of her from his 1831 work '*Letters on Demonologie and Witchcraft*':

"...a gigantic and malignant female...who rode on the storm and marshalled the rambling host of wanderers under her grim banner. This hag...was called Nicneven in that later system which blended the faith of the Celts and of the Goths on this subject. The great Scottish poet Dunbar has made a spirited description of this Hecate riding at the head of witches and good neighbours (fairies, namely), sorceresses and elves,

> *indifferently, upon the ghostly eve of All-Hallow Mass."* (Scott, 1831).

Nicnevin may be associated with or the same as another named being, the Gyre-Carling, who is also sometimes referred to as a queen of Fairy: *"The fairy queen is identified, in popular tradition, with the Gyre-Carline, or mother witch, of the Scottish peasantry. She is sometimes termed Nicneven."* (Scott, 1802). Both Nicnevin and the Gyre-Carling are also closely associated with human witches, who across the early modern period were often connected to or associated with fairies more generally.

Diana – the Roman goddess was named in some sources, including James the VI in the 16th century as a queen of the Scottish fairies:

> *"That fourth kinde of spirites, which by the Gentiles was called Diana, and her wandring court, and amongst vs was called the Phairie (as I tould you) or our good neighboures"*[20] (James I, 1924, p 73).

In context this doesn't seem to have been a named used within Scottish folk belief but rather a name inserted by the intelligentsia recording the material who perhaps felt that Diana was a more familiar name to their readers. Nonetheless I mention it here to provide a more complete picture of the evidence that we have to work with.

Saint[21] **Michael** – There is a great deal of Christian syncretism to be found across folk belief around fairies, and this is true for who the rulers may be as well. Although we have no firm references to Christian figures as rulers of the fairy court(s) we do find strong hints of it within Scottish folk belief. Emma Wilby mentions a possible connection to Archangel Michael as fairy king in her book *The Visions of Isobel Gowdie* where she connects some of Isobel's trial testimony to the idea that both the fairies and Michael had connections in folk belief to militancy, arrows, horses, and flight (Wilby, 2010). In other words, Saint Michael fits the description of the fairy king and was likely, according to Wilby, fit into that role in some syncretic practices. He has found a place in modern belief as the king of fairies as well for some people for the same reasons and because the fairies in some views are seen as angels and Michael is chief of the angels, ergo he is leader of the fairies (Murray, 2024).

Devil as Fairy King – In *Thomas of Erceldoune* the Queen of Fairy strongly disavows any demonic nature or direct connection to Hell,[22] and while the priests might label the Fairy Queen demonic, she is more often compared to the Queen of Heaven in folk material. The same does not hold true, however, for the Fairy King, who seems to exist in a liminal space in folk belief. While he appears in many accounts very clearly described as a being of Fairyland, labelled the king of the elves or the king of the fairies, descriptions of him and his interaction with humans closely align with contemporary ideas of the Devil. Accused witch Margaret Alexander described the king of Fairy as *"a black man dressed in green"*; she claimed that after having sex with him *"his nature was cold"*, reflecting common descriptions of similar encounters with the Devil (Henderson & Cowan, 2007). The description of the fairy king as a black man[23] dressed in green may also echo other accounts of the Devil appearing dressed in green, a colour that had a strong connection to fairies across Scottish folk belief, and which may indicate the blurring of the two concepts, Devil and Fairy King, together (Wilby, 2009). In the 1619 trial of John Stewart the accused claimed to have met a Fairy King in Ireland decades prior who had touched his forehead with a rod which granted him visions; the court then had the spot that had been touched pricked, as would be done for demonic cases, and finding the area lacked sensation saw this as clear evidence of the Devil's influence (Henderson & Cowan, 2007). Although unusual because of her voluntary and detailed testimony, in Isobel Gowdie's accounts of her interactions with spirits she describes the Devil outfitting 'elf boys' with the arrows to make elfshot, overlapping the concepts of the Devil and Fairy King (Henderson & Cowan, 2007; Wilby, 2009). Although she did in other testimony describe a separate king of Fairy the Devil as she described him seemed to act as the power behind the fairies, and perhaps their ultimate authority.

The Scottish Fairy Courts are a complex topic and one that has evolved across centuries. From its initial appearance in folk belief in the 16th and 17th century as a euphemism for all fairies it later grew into a pair of antithetical terms described two groups of fairies, one who favoured humans more and one who very much did not. This dichotomous understanding would take on moral implications into the 19th and 20th centuries with the groups being referred to broadly as the 'good' fairies and the 'bad' fairies as their general attitude towards humanity was extrapolated outwards and assumed to be their wider way of interacting with the human world in general. It is this more recent iteration of the two courts that would, in the late 20th century, be absorbed into urban fantasy and from there become widely popularized, but not without some significant changes.

Chapter 4

Other Cultures

"Bodb king of the fairy-hill of Munster, the other the king of the fairy-hill of Connacht. The fairy-hill of Bodb that is the fairy-hill at Femun. The fairy-hill of Ochaill that is the fairy-hill of Cruachan. There was friendship between the king of the fairy-hill of Munster, and the king of the fairy-hill of Connacht."

De Choppur in Dá Muccida

The concept of the fairy courts as they are widely understood today are deeply rooted in Scottish folk belief, but it is worth exploring how the monarchy of the Otherworld is understood elsewhere, both to show the contrast with the Scottish views and to clarify for those who may have drawn some false conclusions based on the way that a great deal of recent fiction[24] has chosen to apply the Scottish concept to anything and everything fairy. I will gently remind readers here that the idea of the Seelie and Unseelie, and indeed a bifurcation of the fairies into groupings of 'good' and 'bad' is not a concept originally found in other Celtic language speaking cultures, although the wider idea itself isn't entirely unique to Scotland. This chapter is also not meant to be a thorough survey of fairy social structures outside Scotland but merely a sampling to show the ways that these beings are and have been understood across Europe because the pervasive popularity of the Scottish courts has erased these distinctions in popular belief.

Fairy beliefs are beautifully complex and diverse, with various cultures, even those that are related or influenced each other, each having a unique understanding of the subject. I personally believe that studying the nuances of these beliefs can lead to a deeper and fuller understanding of the entire concept and of the fairies themselves. I hope that readers will find the same value as we go through a range of cultural interpretations, from Ireland to Romania. I will also note here as we start that the term fairy used in the contexts, we will be discussing are somewhat controversial and are being used only for ease of communication, as the terms from each culture's language are the better options. However, as it will get too confusing to keep constantly reiterating that, I am only going to say it here and ask readers to apply it throughout this section to all but the English material, where the term fairy comes from.

Fairies are generally thought to live within a monarchy, an idea that is found across an array of western European sources and which often imitates or mirrors the connected human culture through the early modern period. What exactly this monarchy looks like, then, is slightly different between cultures, which is what we will be exploring here. There are some modern ideas around fairy social structure which don't involve monarchy; these are usually systems that appear through 21st century channelled material and which reflect a more utopian or egalitarian social structure and those will be discussed as well, although they are slightly outside the topic of fairy courts, to illustrate the range in beliefs. We will briefly discuss the various iterations of each cultures fairies, and then what we may know about those who are believed to be the monarchs in those places; while this second discussion may seem tangential it is actually important to understand in context who was thought to rule in each place or within each culture's folklore as this is another area where popular culture today has created a great deal of confusion that deserves to be untangled, particularly by often placing the English fairy monarchs over all fairies or explicitly over fairies in cultures which had their own folkloric kings and queens.

Ireland

Irish folk belief does not use the term court, by either definition, for the fairies but they do have a system structured around monarchy which would, by implication, include a royal court. The world of fairy in Ireland is centred on the sidhe, the Otherworldly mounds or hills which connect the human world to the Other, as well as magical islands which may appear in the human world but exist outside of it. In Irish folk belief the Otherworld was originally ruled by the king Manannán from one such island, Emhain Abhlac, but when the Tuatha De Danann, the old Irish gods, went into the sidhe and joined the people there many of the most prominent figures became kings and queens. These figures each rule their own specific domain and have complex relationships with each other which can include both alliances and rivalries. In particular the fairies of different provinces are known to be rivals and to compete over things; in folklore the harvest is a common point of contention with the Good Folk fighting battles in the sky or playing games of skill like hurling to decide which will have the best harvest for the year (MacNeill, 1964). In the mythic tale *De Choppur in Dá Muccida* the competition is based on whose pigs are the best each year. In contrast some other adjoining locations are ruled by spouses or siblings who may be known to have positive relationships with each other and even sometimes act jointly.

A non-exhaustive list of some locations and the king or queen they are associated with (note some have more than one location connected to them or more than one king or queen attributed to them):

Sidhe of Cruachan aka Uaimh na gCat – the Morrigan[25]
Sidhe of Cruachan – Ochall Oichni
Sid in Broga aka Newgrange – Oengus
Brí Leith – Midhir
Emain Macha – Macha

Cnoc Má – Finbhearra
Cnoc Sí Ghabhna – Úna
Sidhe Foinnachaidh – Lir
Cnoc Áine – Áine
Crag Liath – Aoibheall
Carraig Cliodhna – Cliodhna
Sidhe Boidb and Lough Derg – Bodb Dearg
Sidhe al Femen – Bodb Dearg
Emhain Abhlac – Manannán
Tír na nÓg – Manannán
Cnoc Fírinne – Donn Fírinne

In each of these cases we find stories that show that a specific location is thought to be ruled by a king, queen, or much more rarely a pair, and that they in turn are served by those around them which would include warriors, servants, cooks, doorkeepers, cowherds, entertainers,[26] musicians, and poets. The social structure is closest here to medieval or iron age Ireland, even in more recent stories. This structure means that there are various kings and queens as well as one overarching high king, something that was also true in Ireland at different points in history. In the oldest versions this high king would have been Manannán, but after the Tuatha De Danann went into the sidhe the high king of the good folk was said to be the Dagda, an idea referenced in both *Aisligne Oengusso* and *De Gabail in t-Sida*. In some later accounts the Dagda's son Bodb Dearg is referred to as the king of all the sidhe, and in folklore found around Galway his youngest son Finnbheara is given this title (Finnbheara being the fairy king local to Galway in particular so this view there isn't entirely surprising).

In addition to the kings and queens discussed above there is at least one other distinct group of beings within Irish belief which have their own social structure and monarchy: Leprechauns. Although modern folklore has minimized their powers and absorbed them into wider understandings of the sióga [fairies] in older stories and mythology Leprechauns were not solitary shoemakers but a type of water sprite that had the ability to influence many things. In the *Echtra Fergus meic Leiti* and the *Aided Fergus meic Leiti* we learn that Leprechauns live in a complex culture which includes everything from servants to poets to a king and queen. While the Aos Sidhe are usually described as the same size as an average human Leprechauns are about 18 inches [a half meter] tall, and they do not seem to fall into the wider jurisdiction of the Aos Sidhe but to live within their own kingdom.

There is no division of the aos sidhe [people of the sidhe] by moral alignment or by affinity or animosity towards humans, as it is widely understood that they all have the potential to help or to harm. What divisions exist are usually based on area, or on a division by the specific type of being.

Wales

The Welsh Fairy Courts are somewhat unique among those found across Europe as they centre on a King rather than a Queen, and either don't have a queen or she is barely mentioned in stories. There are two different understandings of who the King of Annwfn [the Welsh Otherworld] is, with one focusing on Arawn and the other on Gwyn ap Nudd. In both views, however, this kingship isn't uncontested, with a rival appearing who the king must fight against; there has been some suggestion that this may represent older beliefs around a division of the year into summer and winter with each half ruled by a different figure, however, that is only speculation.

The Welsh structure, like the Irish and the others we will discuss, reflects the human politics of the place the stories grew from. The Welsh Fairy Court is described as a single unified one, although the throne may be contested, and structured so that ultimately one being is perceived as leading it or holding power over those who dwell within Annwfn, perhaps mirroring older ideas of Wales as a single unified country but one which has dealt with outside intrusion and foreign influence.

Arawn is named as the king of Annwfn in the first branch of the Mabinogi where he encounters a human king, Pwyll, and requests Pwyll complete a task for him in compensation for Pwyll killing the deer that Arawn was hunting (Starling, 2024). This task is needed because Arawn has been unable to kill his rival Hafgan, another king of Annwfn, and hopes that Pwyll can succeed where he has failed. Mhara Starling in her book *Welsh Fairies* discusses the dynamic between the two kings, arguing that rather than two kings of one kingdom they represent kings of adjoining kingdoms within Annwfn or that Hafgan may represent a foreign or occupying force. Arawn does have a queen although she is unnamed and has no significant role within the story, beyond being described as beautiful and kind. After Pwyll completes the task that Arawn had set on him, Arawn alone is the king of Annwfn, at least in this story.

Gwyn ap Nudd is the other, and perhaps more well-known king of the Welsh Otherworld, a figure who appears in both older tales and recent folklore in connection with Annwfn and with the Plant Annwfn, the children of Annwfn, a term used for what in English might be called fairies. While Arawn's position is more straightforward and literary, Gwyn is a complex figure who dances the line between pagan and Christian symbolism, and between Arthurian myth and folk tales. He is named as the leader of the Welsh equivalent of the Wild Hunt, who travels across the sky with a pack of Otherworldly hounds. He has also gained popularity outside of Welsh folklore, being incorporated into modern pagan belief. Gwyn's place than is layered and nuanced, and, as Mhara Starling puts it, *"Gwyn has become the chief fairy of Welsh lore"* (Starling, 2024, p38).

Gwyn's earliest appearance is in a 13th century Welsh poem titled *Llyfr Du Caerfyrddin* where he appears on a battlefield accompanied by a hound and riding a white horse, and laments over the deaths of the noble people who have fallen that day (Starling, 2024). He also plays a role in the Arthurian tale of *Culhwch ac Olwen* where he is part of a group with King Arthur attempting to accomplish impossible tasks so that Culhwch can marry Olwen. Gwyn was locked in perpetual battle with Gwythyr ap Greidawl over his sister/lover Creiddylad; the two were tasked by King Arthur to fight on 1 May every year until Judgement Day, at which point whoever won would the fight would also win her hand in marriage (Jones, 2024). Later Gwynn appears in the *Buched Collen*, a tale of saint Collen in which the saint confronts and then banishes Gwyn and his people as demons, after hearing the locals talking of the famous fairy king (Starling, 2024).

As with the Good Folk in other places the Welsh fairies – more properly Plant Annwfn or y Tylwyth Teg – are an ambiguous group who include beings labelled human dead, demons or devils, or fairies in different sources. They tend to be grouped into loose categories based on where they are associated with, but are also treated as a wider general grouping, loyal to or controlled by a King as discussed above.

France

There are an abundance of fairies to be found in French literature, especially medieval and early modern literature, but we do not have the complex monarchy there that we find elsewhere. When fairies do appear they are often female and referred to as 'ladies' indicating an assumed noble social class, and most often they are interacting with human nobility or knights, although that may be an artifact of the material we have to work with which are largely literary. The other main fairy characters we encounter are knights, who appear as antagonists to human characters.

King Arthur is mentioned in some works, such as Huon of Bordeaux or Brune de la Montaigne, as the king of Fairyland or leader of its people, perhaps reflecting the impact of Arthurian stories on medieval France.

French fairy tales do often have fairy queens, usually unnamed. The story *More Beautiful Than A Fairy* by Charlotte-Rose de Caumont de la Force, suggests that the fairy queen, who is the story's antagonist, is named Nabote; the name in French is from a word meaning dwarf or midget.

England

English fairies, as with the others we have already discussed, lived in a society which was structured around a monarchy, with the English version imitating the early modern British culture it is largely drawn from, so that the King and Queen of Fairy are found along with a complex royal court which includes both courtiers and servants (Wilby, 2005). Shakespeare's play *A Midsummer Night's Dream* offers an example of this structure, with the Fairy Queen depicted with a group of loyal attendants and the King with his ever-loyal servant Puck at his command. 18th and 19th century artwork of the story often shows the two royals, either together or separately, surrounded by a throng of fairies which range in both appearance and apparent function. Similarly, Drayton's 17th century poem *Nymphidia* describes the fairy court in the terms familiar to the audience of that time period, with a King and Queen, knights, pages, and servants, and the 18th century *Childe Rowland* describes a Fairyland whose social structure included an Elf King, cowherds and henwives.

The fairy monarchy of England, unsurprisingly, mimics or imitates the human monarchy with a single ruler or pair to rulers over all the country's fairies. Most of the references we have to names for these monarchs come from literary sources rather than older folk belief as such, although the literature becomes the foundation of later folk belief. We also find a greater continuity and timelessness within the English fairy court with only a single named king and three named queens, one of whom was a thinly veiled fictional depiction of the contemporary English Queen of the author's time.

Oberon – Popularized by Shakespeare, Oberon has deeper roots in both French and German folk belief, with the name deriving from Auberon and Alberich meaning 'elf king'[27]. The character initially appears in a 15th century French story *Huon of Bordeaux* where he is described as a king of the fairies who is the size of a three-year-old child but extremely handsome in appearance and who claims to be the son of Julius Caesar (yes, that Caesar) and Morgan la Fey (Harm, Clark, & Peterson, 2015; Briggs, 1976). Shakespeare's 16th century Oberon would retain the crown and throne of the French version but appear in line with wider English folklore which depicted many fairies as tall and regal, and without the famous parentage. This figure would further become popular in magical grimoires of the 16th through 18th centuries where he appears in several sources, invoked under different guises. In one particular text where he is invoked into a crystal he is called on as an angel, reflecting the perhaps changing way that Oberon was understood (Harm, Clark, & Peterson, 2015). In other grimoire material he may be called on to appear as a soldier or child, and invoked to find treasure but he also is able to give knowledge of nature, healing, and invisibility (Harm, Clark, and Peterson, 2015). After this Oberon can be found in various grimoire texts through the 19th century, called on as the king of fairies and also in conjunction with other spirits.

Although there are several named English fairy queens, discussed below, Oberon would be the only king found across older folk belief, paired sometimes with Titania and other times with Mab.

Titania – Shakespeare paired this fairy queen with Oberon, but placed her as somewhat less significant and powerful. In *A*

Midsummer Night's Dream the two contest over possession of a human child that each wants to keep as a servant. To further this end Oberon has Titania cursed so that she falls in love with a feckless human with a donkey head, an act meant to embarrass her for refusing to turn the child over to him. Although Oberon and Titania are shown to be at odds and to command their own personal servants the two are rulers of a single fairy court. Her name seems to be a corrupted form of Diana, who was often associated with supernatural beings and – as we saw in the previous chapter – a name given to the anonymous Fairy Queen by those outside active belief.

Glorianna – A character in Edmund Spenser's 16th century epic poem *The Faerie Queene* Glorianna is widely thought to be a literary allegory of England's Queen Elizabeth I.

Mab – Another character popularized, and possible created,[28] by Shakespeare Mab is described in *Romeo and Juliet* as the fairies' midwife but would later be considered a fairy queen. Unlike the other fairy monarchs Mab is explicitly described as the size of a stone set in a ring and placed firmly within that miniature world, with her coach built from a nutshell and bug parts. She is rarely paired with a king, but in Drayton's 17th century satire *Nymphidia,* Oberon is her husband and king, and is also shrunk down to a tiny size.

The English grimoire material also names a Fairy Queen, although she is otherwise obscure in folk belief. These include Sibilia, Micoll, Titam, and Burfex; we will address what is known of each here.

Sibilia is mentioned as being both the 'empress' and 'princess' of all fairies to whom all others are servants (Harm, Clark, & Peterson, 2015). She appears in two grimoire rituals that I know of, one in an ancillary capacity merely referenced as having dominion over other fairies while in the other she is invoked into a candle flame to reveal the truth and answer questions put to her. Brock and Raiswell mention that she may be invoked along with Milia and Achilia reflecting a pattern sometimes seen of using alliterative names.

Micoll is another commonly invoked fairy Queen. Her name is found under many various spellings including Micol, Mical, Mycholl, Micob, and Mycob as well as Michel and Micheal (Harm, Clark, & Peterson, 2015; Brock & Raiswell, 2018). Under the variant form of Meillia it is possible that Micoll might be the Milia found grouped sometimes with Sibilia, although we more often see her explicitly invoked with Titam and Burfex. Possibly a variant form of Mab, Briggs suggests that Micol is the queen of the diminutive fairies. (Briggs, 1976; Harm, Clark, & Peterson, 2015). Micoll was called on to give knowledge of "herbs, stones...trees...medicines...and the truth" as well as providing a ring of invisibility and was described as being very gentle and kind (Harm, Clark, & Peterson, 2015, page 207).

Often invoked with Micoll are Titam and Burfex. Titam is also called Titem, Tytarit, Titan, Tytan, Tytar, and even Setan or Chicam (Brock & Raiswell, 2018; Harm, Clark, & Peterson, 2015). *The Book of Oberon* suggests that Titam may be connected to or a variant name for Shakespeare's fairy Queen Titania although Briggs argues that Titania is a variant of Diana instead. Because of the obscure nature of the material and the non-standard spelling between sources it is difficult to favour either theory, although it may be that both have some truth in them. Burfex may also be called Burfax, Burphax, or Bursex. Micoll, Titam, and Burfex are invoked together in a ritual to provide the magician with a ring of invisibility, during which one of the three is chosen by the magician and is bound by him to provide him with the ring as well as sexual companionship.

In addition to these named figures, we have a range of references to unnamed monarchs. In the medieval story *Sir Orfeo* and the early modern *Childe Rowland* an Elf King appears and steals a pivotal female character – Orfeo's wife and Rowland's sister, respectively – setting off the action of the subsequent story.

Norse[29]

The Scottish fairies and the culture from which they sprang were influenced by the Norse, via raiding and settlement of Scotland in certain areas; despite this the idea of the Seelie and Unseelie is uniquely Scottish. Because there is an increasing urge in some places to compare or equate the Norse Ljósálfar and Svartálfar with the two Scottish Fairy Courts it is worth discussing here.

Norse álfar, a word that may be translated as elves, are beings who exist in a complex set of beliefs found across Europe from Iceland to Norway, with cognates in Germany and early England. In the oldest source material we currently have, which dates back to the 9th century Anglo-Saxon Leechbooks, these beings are potentially dangerous and associated with various illnesses. In the early Norse material, including the writings of Snorri Sturluson, the álfar are given their own world, álfheim [elf-home], and are often paired with the Gods in phrases indicating that they are a connected but distinct group. However, Sturluson confusingly describes two worlds (of the nine found in Norse cosmology) using the term álfar, Ljósálfheim or light elf home, and Svartálfheim or black elf home; Svartálfheim is said to be the home of the dwarves (Simek, 1993). Jacob Grimm, writing in the 19th century would discuss Sturluson's Ljósálfar and Svartálfar and add in a third group, the Dökkálfar or 'dark elves'. Simek suggests that the Ljósálfar and Sturluson's descriptions of them were influenced by Christian angels and Grimm also suggests that the division of elves into groups reflected a moral judgement, with light elves being angels, black elves demons, and dark elves the human dead in purgatory.

These interpretations reflect foreign influences and filters placed on the material as it was recorded and the actual stories show no such clear moral distinctions with Svartálfar presumably an alternate name for dwarves, Dökkálfar as Grimm himself calls them 'mountain elves' who are often associated with burial mounds, and the Ljósálfar closely connected to the Norse Gods, particularly the Vanir. According to both Sturluson and widespread folk belief, the Vanic God Freyr rules the Ljósálfar. In folk belief through today the álfar are not understood in such a regimented way but are spirits which exist near to humans, occasionally interact with them, and can be either beneficial if respected or dangerous if offended, showing that the actual folk beliefs don't and likely never have aligned with the material recorded by outside scholars.

Considering the structure applied by Sturluson and Grimm, however, it would be tempting to assume that this Norse system and the veneer of Christian interpretation applied to it influenced the Seelie and Unseelie courts but it is best to keep in mind that the Unseelie court is a rather late belief, coming in by the early 19th century, and that for the bulk of recorded belief there was only the Seelie court, which would give lie to any direct comparisons between the two cultures understanding of these beings. As well in Scottish belief, as discussed in Chapter 2, all fairies/elves were understood as demonic by the early modern period which again rendered a close comparison to the Norse beliefs difficult to support. It is more likely that the wider concepts of the álfar combined with existing Celtic cultural understandings of the Sìthe may have influenced Scottish understandings of the elves.

Romania

Romanian fairies represent a fascinating group within wider European fairy belief, both similar to and different from the Scottish. Although their social structure isn't exactly like the monarchies previously discussed, they are generally understood within specific groups, with the Sânziene somewhat comparable to the Seelie court, the Rusalii comparable to the Unseelie and the Zâne as a neutral third group, although Zâne is also simply the term for 'fairy'. The Sânziene are solar aligned beings who are considered somewhat friendlier to humans, while the Rusalii are their more dangerous counterparts; euphemisms are often used for the Rusalii, including 'Iele' which means 'they', 'themselves' (Simina, 2023). The Sânziene are ruled by a queen, Ilena Sânziana, and the Rusalii by a queen named Rusalia; while the Sânziene are most associated with benevolence they can be deadly if offended and similarly while the Rusalii are usually considered dangerous they may also aid in driving out spirits of illness (Simina, 2024).

New Age

Although not a culture per se – more of a subculture – the New Age movement has impacted some modern views on fairy social structure. These ideas in turn were shaped by older views coming from Theosophy, which posited fairies as a less evolved class of spirit shaped and impacted by human belief and interaction. Through the 20th century in this subculture fairies came to be blended with the idea of ascended masters or highly evolved spirits to take on the role of evolved guides to humanity. In John Matthews' channelled material where he claimed to communicate with the sidhe,[30] he described a group of beings that operate as a collective consciousness, without leaders or rank, and who speak with one voice. David Spangler takes a more nuanced approach, describing his sidhe as unified via telepathy but still distinct individuals, and suggesting they live in a mostly egalitarian community where an individual may take a leadership role organically if necessary, based on their own superior ability with the situation at hand. He also says that his sidhe do have a King and a Queen, but that these are not monarchs proper but rather symbols or embodiments of the essence of his sidhe and that they act almost like demi-gods or angels who can inhabit any of the sidhe if needed and can communicate guidance to their people without ruling over them as such. Through this lens the sidhe and fairies more generally are usually viewed as cohabiting in harmony rather than having any government.

Key Take Aways

There are several general statements that can be made about fairy courts across European cultures, because although they are widely different in many ways there are some throughlines between them. These may not apply equally to all and there may also be some few exceptions, but they can be sussed out as general truths.

1. Fairy Queens are more common than Fairy Kings, although both exist in folk belief. While the human world has, throughout history, favoured male rulers and treated queens as something of an aberration until relatively recently, Fairy seems to invert this idea. While fairy kings can be found across folklore one is more likely to find a queen ruling in Fairy than a king; this may reflect an inversion of human social norms something that is widespread in fairy belief. Also, while we find many fairy queens ruling alone, fairy kings are almost always paired with a queen, even when the king is positioned as the primary ruler.
2. Fairies exist in social groups that may be divided by area or social levels – solitary versus trooping, for example – but are only rarely divided by any moral differences. The good folk of these areas' belief can be helpful or harmful to humans but do not exist within groupings that are entirely one or the other.

3. Fairy hierarchy most often reflects the human hierarchy connected to them. In cultures that traditionally have or have had a strong emphasis on monarchy we find stories of fairies with queens and kings. In places or more modern iterations of belief where rigid social structures are rejected or egalitarianism is idealized, we find stories of fairies which reflect this as well.

Chapter 5
Gaming

"They are two sides of the same coin, or let us say . . . the same side of two coins."

Tom Stoppard, Rosencrantz and Guildenstern are Dead

Role-Playing Games or RPGs are group-oriented games based in storytelling and can include either Table Top Role-Playing Games or TTRPGs or Live Action Role-Playing, or LARP. Both kinds of games have incorporated the Seelie and Unseelie courts in different ways and to different extents as games expanded to include more variety and began to draw on folklore for inspiration. Before we dive into the ways that some of these games have incorporated the courts we must perforce begin with a basic outline of what these games are and what they can involve to establish the groundwork that the more detailed material is growing from. As there are many possible variations within these games I am focusing, as usual, on the broader strokes and on the specific games which include the courts in some fashion.

Modern role-playing began, as such, with Dungeons and Dragons (D&D) which was founded in 1974 and followed up with Advanced Dungeons and Dragons in 1978. The 1980s saw an explosion in RGPs and in 1987 the Forgotten Realms setting was added to D&D, expanding into an area where the fae and courts were featured in a wider way. This would be followed in 1995 by a LARP through White Wolf Publishing[31] called Changeling: The Dreaming in which the courts were a pivotal aspect of the game. These represent the main games that feature the fairy courts and which are popular enough to have had a noticeable effect on wider belief.

These games may be set in fantasy worlds or in alternate versions of Earth, and have long drawn on older folklore and concepts as sources to build from. RPGS are usually run by one or two people who take the role of storyteller or 'dungeon master'; these people create the storylines for the players to engage with which are often quest based.[32] Storytellers/ Dungeon Masters may also either take on or narrate the roles of Non-Playable Characters (NPCs); these are the characters within the story that players encounter and interact with as they go through their adventure and can include enemies that are being fought against, allies, or neutral parties.

Role-playing games generally allow a person to create a playable character which can be human or may be one of a variety of other types of beings (depending on the game) including in some games different kinds of fairies. Each character will also have specific skill sets and roles, things like druid, paladin or warlock, for example, as well as a backstory which can be as simple or complex as the player wants. Character stats like strength, intelligence, charisma, agility, and wisdom are based on dice rolls and effected by the species the person has chosen, with some species having bonuses for specific stats. This all allows for a great deal of personalization of characters by players and creates a sense of ownership over the character as well as an inherent connection between player and character. This is even truer with people who live action role-play as they are embodying their character in improv style interactions with other players.

One aspect of gaming which is pertinent to understanding how the fae folk and fairy courts appear and act is the moral alignment system that most RPGs use. This system broadly divides morality into nine categories based on two sets of three groupings: good, neutral, and evil; and lawful, neutral and chaotic. This results in nine playable moral alignments: lawful good, neutral good, chaotic good, lawful neutral, true neutral, chaotic neutral, lawful evil, neutral evil, and chaotic evil. Good characters choose the outcome that is best for the most people, neutral characters what is best under the circumstances, evil characters what is best for themselves. Lawful characters follow the letter of the law, chaotic characters do whatever they decide in the moment, and neutral characters as implied are neutral between law and chaos. A lawful evil character, for example, would enforce and support laws which benefit themselves to the detriment or outright harm of others, while a lawful good character would follow the law for the greatest good. Fairies are often described through this system as chaotic neutral because they are somewhat unpredictable and prone to valuing personal relationships over community (good) or self (evil). Through this lens the Seelie court would be considered lawful good and the Unseelie lawful evil.

D&D

Dungeons and Dragons includes a wide array of playable worlds and characters which are under a constant system of expansion and revision. One aspect of this is a place called the Feywild which functions as a world within the world of D&D and is based at least loosely on folklore about Fairy. Within this concept are creatures called the fey[33] who exist in two courts the Seelie and Unseelie; the Seelie are the more prominent group and can act as both demi-gods within the game or the court itself can be a playable setting, while the Unseelie are malicious and enjoy causing harm to anyone they can (Ashif, 2024). The D&D Seelie court is ruled by Titania while the Unseelie court is ruled by her sister the Queen of Air and Darkness; Oberon is also named as the king of the Seelie court although he features less prominently and it is the two queens who actually rule (Kestrel & Price, 2002; Ashif, 2024). Within gameplay the seelie are considered to be neutral or neutral good characters while the unseelie are chaotic neutral or chaotic evil, although both groups are considered unpredictable and with at least some chaotic behaviours (Ashif, 2024). The seelie court is highly restricted, accepting only its own members and those connected to it, while the Unseelie are open to anyone with any degree of fey ancestry, creating courts which are not only morally opposed to each other but also vastly different in how they approach other beings (Kestrel & Price, 2002).

The D&D versions of the two courts are designed around the functionality of game play and are tailored to that setting with entirely fictional backstories, in this case that the seelie court once had its own world which was destroyed by the dark magic of the unseelie creating the current state of things. The Seelie and Unseelie of D&D are more directly opposed to each other than what is found in folklore. In general, the fey folk of D&D are thought of as both beings from a different reality and beings who are intrinsically connected to the natural world (Kestrel & Price, 2002). The D&D understanding of the courts is also the basis for the *Forgotten Realms* understanding of them.

Forgotten Realms

The Seelie court in *Forgotten Realms* game play is also called the Summer Court and are the gods of the fey folk; ruled by Titania they existed within an inner and outer court (Gray, 2014). Much of the structure and understanding of the seelie court is built off of existing material in D&D, but tailored to the specific setting of the *Forgotten Realms*. As a pantheon of gods, the Seelie generally don't interact directly with this world but may serve as patrons to players connected to a specific pantheon, as well as any fey character. The Unseelie court may also be called the Gloaming Court and existed in opposition to the Seelie, ruled by Titania's sister the Queen of Air and Darkness (Sargent, 1992). While the Seelie exist as forces of good the Unseelie are evil and their actions are generally aimed at causing suffering; as with the wider D&D understanding the Unseelie will take in anyone with any fey blood and are known to even accept monsters.

Changeling: The Dreaming

The game which has had possibly the greatest effect on modern perceptions of the two courts is *Changeling* by White Wolf. A LARP Changeling allows players to create and embody characters who are members of one court or the other. The game is set in a human world where the supernatural is real and interactive, connected to or inhabited by beings – fairies – from a world called Arcadia. The game includes a variety of named fairy beings from folklore and also includes the two Scottish Fairy Courts as universal concepts, although as we will discuss the courts are portrayed in very different ways from what exists in folklore.

In *Changeling* the fae originated in a world called Arcadia, or the Dreaming, and exist by absorbing the energy of human dreams or 'glamour'. The nobility of the fae, called the sidhe, withdrew into Arcadia as rational thought in the human world began to weaken glamour and create something called 'banality' which injured the fae. This withdrawal resulted in two different groups of fae, the nobility and the commoners. Eventually the combined weakening of glamour and rise of banality caused a break between realities and resulted in the commoner fae creating a ritual that allowed them to take over a human body to live within the human world; this possession is what created changelings. This process involved a fae soul taking over a human body and displacing the original soul, while simultaneously existing within the Dreaming, creating a human embodied fae. During the modern period of human history dreams returned and with them the sidhe, who joined the commoner fae in creating changelings to interact with the human world. During gameplay a character must try to increase their glamour while avoiding banality as much as possible.

Each changeling would be aligned with either the seelie or unseelie courts and would belong to a 'kith' which is effectively the specific type of fairy that the character is. Examples of kiths include pooka, redcaps, sidhe or boggans. The court alignment and kith shape the characters personality and actions during game play. Game play emphasizes the complexity of court politics, with various noble houses a character can be affiliated with which also effect the character, inner and outer courts, kingdoms, and assorted other groups. The backstory also emphasizes the tension between sidhe and commoner fae, as well as the power plays and struggles that are common between groups (Howard, 1995).

While loosely based in folklore the majority of *Changeling* material is highly fictionalized and creative. While we can perhaps argue for some slight moral distinction between the two groups in how they would approach humans, the differences between courts in the game is based on their philosophy of life. The Seelie court of *Changeling* is based on historic concepts around love and honour, including old codes of chivalry, while the Unseelie embrace passion and novelty; the seelie consider the unseelie crass and unpredictable while the unseelie view the seelie as stodgy and honour-bound. The motto of the seelie court is: Love conquers all, death before dishonour, beauty is life, and never forget a debt; while the Unseelie motto is: change is good, glamour is free, honour is a lie, passion before duty (Brucato, 1996). Historically the two courts divided the rule of the year into summer and winter and were open enemies but after the entrance of changelings to the world and the need for both groups to fight against banality they have at least theoretically made peace with each other (Woodworth, 1998). Currently in game reality the Seelie court is the dominant power with the Unseelie reduced to a Shadow Court, but both exist as playable character options.

Changeling: The Lost

Following up on *The Dreaming* in 2007 White Wolf released *Changeling: The Lost* which featured playable characters who had once been human but were kidnapped by the fae and changed, before escaping back to earth where they seek to avoid recapture and return to the fae world. In contrast to *The Dreaming's* fae souled, human bodied characters *The Lost* features characters who were fully human and changed by magic into something partially fae. The changelings of *The Lost* are at odds with mortals, as they no longer properly belong to that world, but also with the full fae who are responsible for their current state.

The court system of *The Lost* is much more complex than what we find in *The Dreaming*. European and western culturally based changelings belong to one of four seasonal courts summer, fall, winter, or spring, while eastern European and Slavic changelings have two courts, sun and moon, and Asian based changelings have four courts based in the directions; additionally, there is the dawn and dusk courts as well as the courtless. The second edition of the players handbook expanded the directional courts from four to five, added the three rose courts as well as two courts of creation (Cochrane, 2018). The courts in *The Lost* are groups that have come together based in a shared interest or focus and have made an agreement with the power their court is named after so that that power will protect them from the full fae (Cochrane, 2018).

Gaming changed how some people interacted with the concepts of the fairy courts, by allowing them to embody characters who were members of these groups. In the same way that urban fantasy changed how readers understood and engaged with this material gaming was in many ways a paradigm shift, particularly for neopagans. RPGs, especially *Changeling*, had a strong impact as well on the Otherkin[34] community which predates these games but has since, in at least some demographics, incorporated terms from the games including kith, kithain, and arcadia. The Unseelie motto from *Changeling* has been repeated unironically within discussions as a genuine aspect of both belief and folklore.[35] The D&*D Feywild* has also found a place within some modern pagan groups who may also embrace the concepts around cold iron found within the game, indicating perhaps both the overlap between the gaming and pagan communities as well as the way that people outside cultures with living fairy beliefs are incorporating material from popculture instead. The folklore that is espoused by some people now is rooted in 20th century gaming but more often than not is assumed to be genuinely older cultural material, contributing to a growing widespread misunderstanding of the Scottish Fairy Courts.

Chapter 6
Urban Fantasy

"We changed the names of the two fey armies to the Summer and Winter courts. Seelie and Unseelie are traditional in Britain, but the Folk are in America now, after all. And we wanted the names to reinforce the characters of the two groups: one concentrated on growing, the other one dying..."

Emma Bull, appendix discussing writing a screenplay version of the novel War For The Oaks

For hundreds of years the idea of two fairy courts or groups was mostly limited to the Lowland areas of Scotland, however, this began to change in the late 20th century with the advent of a new genre – urban fantasy. The genre focuses on stories that include supernatural or paranormal characters or concepts within an urban setting. Similar stories that aren't city focused are sometimes lumped into urban fantasy and sometimes distinguished as contemporary fantasy, while plots that feature or centre romance or erotica may be labelled as paranormal romance; there is a great deal of fluidity and overlap between these subcategories. Urban fantasy has precedents in novels and short stories across the 20th century but the term didn't come into popular use until the 1970s and the genre didn't truly take shape until the 1980s. Terri Windling's 1986 *'Borderland'* and Emma Bull's 1987 *'War for the Oaks'* are usually referenced as foundational works within urban fantasy and some of the earliest recognizable modern stories to feature folkloric beings including elves and fairies in an urban, technological setting. While fairies have appeared as characters in fiction for centuries this new approach to fantasy would mark both a popularization of the terms seelie and unseelie as well as an eventual rewriting of the concepts which has had a strong impact on how the courts are understood outside Scottish folklore. Urban fantasy took the lowland Scots' fairy courts and turned them into a general affiliation for all beings considered fairies, or in current terms, fae.[36] The words were also divorced from their underlying meanings which allowed authors creative liberties that those familiar with the definitions might disagree with. There is perhaps also an argument for some cultural appropriation here, as the terms were taken and used outside the source culture without concern for their original context, but there is an equal argument that the original usage in fiction did mostly adhere to the folkloric and was only slowly eroded away by subsequent authors who were each trying to put their own twist on the concept for their own audiences. I will let readers draw their own conclusion as to that.

Urban fantasy in the late 1980's and 1990s which included fairies initially adhered to the older understandings of who these beings were and depicted them as chiefly amoral from a human perspective but having factions which were more well inclined towards humans and factions that were more antagonistic. In Emma Bull's 1987 work '*War for the Oaks*' the two Scottish courts are ubiquitous affiliations for all of the Fair Folk and the protagonist, who lives in the United States, encounters both the groups in the story. It is worth noting that in the urban fantasy depictions the two courts are not seen as two loose groups defined by their approach to humanity but as two groups loyal to Fairy Queens who lead, and in many ways embody, their groups creating a system that is closer to a modern political party or nation than the previous folkloric view. Bull's fairies are generally in line with the folklore she is pulling from, with her Unseelie clearly of a more malevolent nature and her Seelie not wholly benevolent beings; rather they are depicted as callous towards humanity and willing to use an innocent human to their own ends even if it results in the human's death. Bull's main fairy character, the Phouka, describes the Seelie court as *"[the] noblest blood of Faerie, the guardians, the rulers"* in contrast to the Unseelie who he describes as the commoners compared to the noble Seelie, although the story shows that each group has a Queen (Bull, 1987, p 250). Bull depicts the Unseelie as more inclined to harm than the Seelie but doesn't paint the Seelie as overly benevolent either, with the exception of the Phouka. In Mercedes Lackey's 1992 book *'Born to Run'* and subsequent *SERRAted Edge* series we find the Seelie and Unseelie as the main supernatural groups with her version of elves, also called by the Irish term sidhe in the book, being described as largely inhuman in their emotions and actions. Unlike Bull's approach, however, Lackey gives a much stronger morality to her fairies, although one that operates above and largely beyond humanity, with her Seelie being distinctly good and her Unseelie unmitigatingly cruel; in a sense Lackey's Seelie and Unseelie are concentrated versions of what's found in older folklore, distilled into their extremes for her narrative purposes. Her Seelie court are primarily represented by elves who are described as being from Ireland[37] and who are interested with engaging with the human world, albeit in secrecy, and who are also focused on earning money to donate to human charities, especially those which help children. In contrast Lackey's Unseelie court are focused on causing as much harm and misery in the human world as possible, while also targeting the Seelie court who they are both subtly and overtly at war with. Both Bull and Lackey envision the two courts as not only philosophically opposed to each other but also martially opposed, depicting them as enemies either, as Bull describes it, because of a deep-seated animosity towards each other, or as Lackey would have it, because their philosophical difference put them in direct conflict with each other's goals and activities in the human world.

As urban fantasy has moved into the 21st century the depiction of fairies, of various types and by various names, has evolved noticeably. The clear delineations between Seelie and Unseelie found in the earlier iterations of the genre have given way to much more fluid and flexible depictions. In Laurell K Hamilton's book *Kiss of Shadows*, published in 2000, the Seelie and Unseelie beyond the names are largely interchangeable with both being dangerous and manipulative. Hamilton forwards the idea that the Unseelie are not actually more dangerous to humanity than their Seelie counterparts and are the more honest, accepting, and straightforward of the two courts. While initially appearing in conflict with the protagonist it is quickly apparent that the majority of Unseelie characters in the story are heroic in nature, acting to protect the protagonist and showing care and concern for her personally. In Holly Black's 2002 book *Tithe* the two courts are morally indistinguishable, with both Queens depicted as capricious and cruel, and the courts themselves as royal courts which pressed other fairy beings into service, as the author describes them through dialogue in the text:

> *"Once, there were two low courts, the bright and the dark, the Seelie and the Unseelie, the folk of the air and the folk of the earth. They fought like a serpent devouring its own tail, but we kept from their affairs, kept to our hidden groves and underground streams, and they forgot us. Then they made a truce and remembered that rulers must have subjects..."* (Black, 2002, p 79).

As with Hamilton's work, Black ultimately depicts characters among the Unseelie court, notably the knight Roiben, as the more trustworthy and heroic as opposed to the Seelie who actively work harm against the protagonist and her friends. Although the Unseelie here are still depicted as dangerous they are clearly positioned in line with the protagonist and in empathetic ways.

Both of these examples are in stark contrast to older folklore and to the late 20th century works of Bull and Lackey where the Unseelie are unquestionably the antagonists.

The 21st century books show a wider pattern of sympathizing with and ultimately depicting fairies of the Unseelie court as the actual heroes while the fairies of the Seelie court take on the role of the villains. Ron C Nieto's *Faery Sworn* series which begins with the 2014 book *Wild Hunt* adheres more closely, in general, to folklore but also leans into the idea that the Seelie are the more dangerous court and the Unseelie the more sympathetic; the stories' main character is trying to find and rescue her kidnapped grandmother and her first ally in this is an Unseelie being who helps her realize that the Seelie are the threat she is ultimately fighting, with the Unseelie as her allies. This echoes the tone of both Hamilton and Black's work and pivots strongly away from older and current folk belief. In Sarah J Maas's 2015 book *A Court of Thorns and Roses,* as well as the subsequent books in the series, we find the terms Seelie and Unseelie have been left in favour of new names for a multitude of fairy courts, including the Night Court which takes the role of the Unseelie, but this pattern of presenting a good grouping which is later revealed to be the dangerous ones and introducing a dangerous group which turns out to be heroic holds true.

Most of our focus in this chapter has been on novels, and indeed novels are fertile ground for the subject and a main way that these ideas have been popularized. It is worth noting here that there are other forms of urban fantasy that have also incorporated and spread the fairy courts, most notably perhaps via multimedia and particularly television. Although not as popular there as in written urban fantasy there certainly has been some impact which is worth discussing, particularly via the Canadian television show *Lost Girl*. The show began in 2010 and ran for five seasons, centring on a woman named

Bo who had grown up in the human world but found out she was actually a succubus, which in the show's reality is considered a type of fae. *Lost Girl's* fairies are rigidly divided between the 'Light' and the 'Dark' which are clearly modelled after the Seelie and Unseelie. The Light consist of 10 clans, with the leader of the Light clan in the show named the Ash because Light fae leaders take names from sacred trees. The Light fae are predatory towards humans but only as a necessity and often act to protect them when possible. In contrast the 'Dark', effectively the Unseelie, enjoy being predators and embrace using their powers for their own gain with no regard for humans; they are ruled by the Morrigan, although this represents a name that was taken with the role rather than that person's actual name. Using the terms light and dark reflect a wider pattern of renaming the courts that will be discussed in more depth in the next chapter, but by the point the show was created it had been done across multiple popular book series making the terms seelie and unseelie effectively synonymous with light and dark so that the usage of the terms in *Lost Girl* reflects an established pattern.

The term seelie court evolved from a euphemism into the idea of two opposing courts, one which was more kindly inclined towards humans and one which was malevolent in nature. This double court system found in Scottish folklore eventually spread to modern American fiction where it was further developed not as part of a living belief system but within creative storylines and plot points. In a very short space of time, roughly three decades, we see the traditional Seelie and Unseelie being renamed and those names shifting the understanding of the two courts in subtle ways and eventually less subtle ways. The idea of a third group or court is added by the turn of the 21st century which encompasses those that don't belong to the two main groups. As we get further into the first decade of the 21st century we see the idea of multiple courts, varying in number, of increasing complexity. With the changes to how the courts are understood is a change in how fairies themselves are portrayed and understood, both reflecting and influencing wider popculture beliefs about fairies. As we continue into the 21st century it remains to be seen if the fracturing of the court system continues or stabilizes.

The first adaptation that can be seen in fiction is a shift from using the Scots names to more descriptive terms for each court. Initially the Seelie court started to be called the Bright or Light court while the Unseelie was called the Dark court, something that can be found at least as far back as the late 1980's and early 1990's. Mercedes Lackey's urban fantasy is one example of this with both her *Bedlam Bards* and *SERRAted Edge* series including the traditional names for the courts as well as the modified names, used interchangeably. It is a subtle shift and perhaps understandable as the idea of the courts became popular in a mainstream culture largely detached from traditional fairylore and unfamiliar with the Scots language, but as is often the case when a word in one language is changed to a word in another the connotations changed. The meanings of seelie and unseelie are complicated but are only indirectly moral. Seelie can mean blessed but it does not literally mean godly or morally good; indeed, those meanings would not and could not apply to the Scottish seelie fairies which are as likely to harm as help depending on motivation. And the word unseelie can mean ungodly but it lacks the heavier associations of true devilry or diabolism. Changing the names to 'bright' and 'dark' while more evocative in English does carry a stronger moral implication because of the way that the English language, and modern American culture, have come to associate bright with moral goodness and dark with moral badness. This choice began to shift the understanding of the Courts as well as the beings within them.

Moving into the 21st century we begin to see shifting to seasonal names, initially summer and winter. The Seelie court becomes the Summer court and the Unseelie court becomes the Winter court. This in effect neatly dodges the moral implications entirely which can on the surface seem like a good thing, but in reality has caused a variety of issues. The biggest of which has been the continued erosion of the dangers of Fairy, once well established in folklore, and particularly a softening of the attitude around the Unseelie beings. Books that favour the term Winter Court may still cast that court as the more dangerous of the two but often place their hero or their main characters love interest in that court. One example of this would be the *Faerie Sworn* series by Ron C Neito; the first book *Wild Hunt* was published in 2014, and favours the terms Summer and Winter court with the main character's main allies coming from the Winter court. This sets up an unavoidable system in which the beings who should be the most dangerous instead become, to some degree, the most sympathetic. Whereas the creatures of the old Unseelie court delighted in their viciousness and took pleasure in tormenting humans the beings of this new Winter court are often described as one would a natural predator, simply doing what they do and easily avoided or dealt with by someone who is canny enough. This particular shift in approaching the courts represents a notable departure from traditional folklore.

Further to this shift to a seasonal approach we see continued adaptations to the system itself. For example, the *Dresden Files* novels by Jim Butcher feature a system of fairy courts, introduced into the series in 2002 with the novel *Summer Knight*. In Butcher's novels there are two main courts, the Summer and Winter. Butcher's system also includes so-called 'wyldfae' or unaffiliated beings who belong to neither court but will join one or the other in times of war. This inclusion of a third unaffiliated group marks a new evolution in how the courts are viewed although the idea itself isn't entirely novel. Butcher also hints at the possibility of seasonal courts for spring and autumn which were subsumed by the two main courts, although this is an idea that is fleshed out far more on fan sites than in Butcher's own writing.

The idea of two main Courts with a third more neutral option is also one we see in other works of modern fiction. In Dana Maria Bell's erotica series, which began in 2009, there are three Courts: the black, white, and grey. The black is roughly synonymous with the Unseelie, the white with the Seelie, and the Grey are the more neutral beings who do not identify as wholly dangerous nor wholly benevolent. Although it should be noted that Bell's White Court is possibly the most dangerous of the three despite its reputation as the 'good' court. This also reflects a modern trend, to make the renamed Unseelie the better people by some measure and the renamed Seelie the worse, swapping the traditional trustworthiness of each group in some sense. We see this not only with Bell's work but with a variety of others including Laurel K Hamilton's *Merry Gentry* series and many of the works in the young adult genre aimed at teenagers.

Increasingly more complex Court systems in fiction also exist such as we see in the *Court of Thorns and Roses* series by Sarah J Maas, published in 2015. Maas offers seven distinct courts which also include a few sub-courts. The seven main ones are: Spring, Summer, Autumn, Winter, Dawn, Day, and Night. Her choice to base her courts on the four season plus three times of day appears to echo the pattern of change begun with renaming the Seelie and Unseelie after summer and winter, simply taken to a further extreme.

A second distinct feature of the evolution of fairies in urban fantasy across the last several decades is the notable anthropomorphising they have undergone. This recasting of the Good Neighbours into humanized magical beings is an underlying feature of their change from dangerous and mercurial beings into relatable and empathetic characters. This echoes a trend seen in paranormal romance, a closely related genre, by Dr. Bill Hughes who notes in his paper 'Demon Lovers': "*The monster has become tamed, domesticated, or feminised, and transformed into the lover.*" (Hughes, 2014, p2). In urban fantasy we have seen this across the example novels with the way that the Unseelie have begun as intractable enemies inimical to humanity and slowly transformed across the genre into the romantic and heroic figures in contrast to the now deceptive and dangerous Seelie.

When we look over the span of time this discussion has encompassed you will note two crucial things. The initial evolution of the two-court system within Scottish culture was a slow and organic process which occurred over hundreds of years. It was also a process which occurred within a culture that had an inherent and ingrained belief in the Fair Folk during the process. Yes, there was certainly change and we can see how that change progressed, but it was not sudden nor divorced from actual belief. In contrast the recent evolutions or changes in views relating to the courts have been both swift, often happening within less than a decade, and also are rooted in fiction that is not coming from a culture that believes intrinsically in fairies as an objective reality. Certainly, we must at least consider the effect of modern technology and media on the speed of this process.

A final aspect of the fairy courts of urban fantasy must be mentioned here, before we move on and that is who is thought to rule them. This has also changed and evolved over time, and offers no cohesive agreement as different authors have named different folkloric figures, deities, or original characters but there are some discernible patterns, and it can be said that the folkloric figures are generally drawn from English literature which has passed into folklore and the deities from Celtic belief.

Here we will look at a sample of these, drawn from various novels across the last three decades.

War for the Oaks – in this book the Queens are never named but referred to by generic titles: the Seelie queen is called 'the Lady' and the Unseelie Queen 'the Dark Lady'. The Unseelie Queen is also called the 'Queen of Air and Darkness' a reference to a 1922 poem *Her Strong Enchantments Failing* by AE Housman.

SERRAted Edge series – the Queen of the Unseelie court is the Morrigan who is described as a vicious hateful creature who even despises her own people, while the Seelie court is ruled by King Oberon. In later books in the series it is implied that Oberon is the ultimate ruler of all of the sidhe and both courts.

A Kiss of Shadows and the Merry Gentry series – the king of the Seelie is Taranis and the Unseelie Queen is Andais although she also goes by the title of Queen of Air and Darkness. Later in the series a third court is added, ruled by the protagonist. Taranis in mythology is a Gaulish god associated with thunder, while Andais is described in the series as a former war goddess.[38]

The Dresden Files – although using the names Summer and Winter court instead of Seelie and Unseelie, the descriptions of each are the same. The Winter court is ruled by Mab and the summer court by Titania. Mab is also known as the Queen of Air and Darkness, while Titania bears titles like Lady of Light and Life and Queen of the Evergreen.

Tithe and the Modern Faery Tales series – The Queen of the Unseelie is initially Nicnevin, although after her the rulership passes to the main male character of the series, Roiben. The Seelie Queen is Silarial, who later gives her crown to Rioben's sister Eithne as part of a wider plot against him, but when

Eithne is mortally wounded, she names Roiben as the new king of the Seelie, effectively uniting the two courts.

Faery Sworn – the queens are never named but referred to only by titles. This follows a wider pattern in this series wherein names give someone power over a person and titles are generally used in their place.

In an informal survey conducted on social media I found that the most common names mentioned for rulers of the two courts were drawn from Shakespeare, with *The Dresden Files* often cited as a source. Oberon is the most commonly mentioned fairy king, perhaps indicating the place he has found in popculture. The original concepts from Scottish folk belief have been largely lost in modern fiction, or perhaps I should say overwritten.

We should consider the profound impact that this material has had on belief in fairies, especially outside areas and cultures which still have a living folk belief of the subject. Among those who are seeking to connect to fairies and fairy belief or incorporate those beliefs into their own spirituality it seems to be increasingly common to look to modern fiction as a source rather than established folk belief. This is a tricky discussion which must be approached carefully because fiction has always had a place influencing folk belief as much of the material covered in previous chapters shows. What people read for pleasure impacts what they believe and contributes to the spread of these ideas far afield. While we don't often stop and think about it, fiction influences people, sometimes profoundly. This is why people try to ban books, to control the narrative that others are exposed to and in doing so to control the beliefs of those people (Puchner, 2018). For one example of this, a 2017 study 'Human Culture and Science Fiction' looked at the ways that science fiction had impacted science and scientists in the real world, concluding that fiction could both create an interest in a subject that fuelled further research while also creating false, sometimes harmful, understandings of the subject by those outside of it which had real world consequences (Menadue and Cheer, 2017). It can also be seen in the ways that Westernized stories and fiction have demonstrably affected non-Western cultures. Fiction is often more impactful than nonfiction because it creates an empathetic bond between the reader and character so that the reader feels that they are part of the story rather than observing it, and can come to embrace messages and themes within the story as things that personally matter to the reader (Gow, 2012). Stories are carriers of cultures and of belief; when they are creating new beliefs those beliefs can become widespread, such as we see, for example, with Barrie's Tinkerbell who became the template of popculture fairies. For the fairy courts this can be demonstrated by two personal anecdotes. When I was in Armagh in 2016, at the Navan Fort and Centre, re-enactors were retelling an Irish myth in which a fairy man cursed a fairy woman into the shape of a deer for rejecting his advances, and although the concepts of the two courts are entirely foreign to Irish folk belief the story teller referred to the fairy man as 'unseelie'. Then, a few years ago, I asked on social media for people's recommendations for sources on fairy folklore, and more than half of the people who answered suggested urban fantasy books or series.[39]

Fiction Meets Belief

These evolving depictions of fairies in urban fantasy and paranormal romance can perhaps best be described as folkloresque. Foster, in his introduction to the book *The Folkloresque* describes the concept this way: "*the folkloresque is popular culture's own perception and performance of folklore*" (Foster & Tolbert, 2016, p5). In urban fantasy this is seen through the depictions of fairies and related beings which draw on folklore but vary from it as the plot of the story demands and the author's imagination suggests; a true picture of folkloric fairies isn't given then but rather a distorted image filtered through the lens of fiction and the demands of the market. Further to this point Foster describes one example of a movie which pulls on folklore as a source as:

> *"[it is] itself not folklore. As a commercially created product it exists in a fixed form that neither exhibits variation through time and space nor changes with each performance....it was shared with people through formal, institutional channels rather than the informal, person-to-person models most commonly associated with folklore."* (Foster & Tolbert, 2016, p3).

This accurate description applies equally to the folkloresque material found across urban fantasy and paranormal romance, which may incorporate folklore as source material but is a commercial product written for a market and which reaches people through published texts rather than oral storytelling. However, while this material is a popular culture interpretation of folklore it in turn has a tangible influence on beliefs, particularly among people who have no strong grounding in existing fairy folklore or who are separate from cultures that still retain active belief, who in short have no access to traditional folklore but look instead to modern multimedia. These new beliefs, rooted in fiction, then recycle back into fiction as new authors whose knowledge of folklore comes from the folkloresque incorporate this view into their own written stories eventually evolving into a modern popular culture folklore with diverse roots. One example of this cycle of the folkloresque reinforcing itself and then becoming belief may be artistic, theatrical, and fictional depictions of small fairies with wings which are at odds with folkloric fairies that have long been wingless and flown through magic but have become so ubiquitous in mass media that they are now being reported in 20th and 21st century anecdotal accounts of fairy encounters (Young, 2016; 2017).

The current folkloresque understanding of fairies based in modern fiction is the culmination of the wider pattern of romanticizing these beings and of anthropomorphizing them that can be found in literature and among those coming from outside traditions of belief but seeking to revive those beliefs. Dr. Sabina Magliocco discusses these trends in her papers 'Taming the Fae' and 'Reconnecting to Everything' noting particularly the affects among neopagans who seek to actively incorporate fairies into their belief systems and who are more prone to looking at literature as a primary source and of blending literature with folk belief to form a syncretic view. In the first paper she argues that oral traditions are intrinsically connected to literary ones in these groups and that the gentler Victorian and Edwardian views of fairies directed the understanding of these beings away from the more dangerous ones of traditional folklore (Magliocco, 2019, pp 107-108). In the latter paper she discusses the intentional revival of fairy beliefs which is described as *"filtered through literary and ethnographic portrayals of fairies, and romanticized because these narratives reflect a longing for an imagined past"* (Magliocco, 2018, p 329). The fairies of these new neopagan beliefs then are formed from diverse sources across media, from modern fiction, the folkloresque, and older folklore, and amalgamated to create a unique understanding filtered through mainstream Western culture. This view is heavily influenced as well by the idealization of the rural and the natural which is embedded in modern paganism from the Victorian era in which it first began gestating, adding another layer to the way that fairies are understood by this group (Magliocco, 2019). Relevant to urban fantasy these influences are played out by stories which incorporate modern themes and motifs, including the romantic anti-hero, blended with the author's idealized post-Victorian concepts of the fairies they are including. These fairies, particularly the more dangerous Unseelie variety, embody the stereotypical outsider who is rejected by the majority but actually has the greatest value. Dr. Hughes describes an aspect of this we find in paranormal romance while discussing the use of fairies to embody the outsider: *"This connects with the rise of identity politics and the use of the sympathetic monster as representing an Other who is to be engaged in dialogue with rather than excommunicated."* (Hughes, 2014, p21). The dangerous Unseelie antagonist then becomes the heroic and romantic antihero who aids the protagonist's journey throughout the story and often becomes the main love interest after which the hero quests. In turn, as Magliocco outlines in depth in her work, these literary beliefs are taken into popular belief and become the new understanding of fairies for people divorced from cultural folklore.

The result of all of this is that the fairies of neopagan belief represent a blend of idealized elements from diverse sources, including theosophy and the new age movement, but also heavily drawn from literature both historic and modern, creating a new layer of folklore that is unique and diverse, but in which the role of modern urban fantasy should not be underestimated. Belief drawn from fiction feeds on itself, looking for reinforcement in additional literature, and perpetuating in digital media which will forward plotlines from novels and role-playing games into discussions of spirituality and belief. The intertwining trends within urban fantasy of re-envisioning and redefining the Seelie and Unseelie are thus reflected and supported in these communities of belief which similarly see trends of rehabilitating and softening the Unseelie; an example can be found in DJ Conway's book *Moon Magic*, a work aimed at a neopagan audience, which suggests that the Unseelie are not dangerous – in fact do no more than make humans feel uneasy – and should be approached in a friendly manner (Conway, 2002). This idea, which reflects the trends across urban fantasy of disempowering the dangerous fairies and anthropomorphizing them, becomes a facet of the entire belief system that incorporates fairies in this new context. This is a stark and clear contrast with older interactions between witches and fairies which could be congenial in some contexts but were always relationships dictated and controlled by the fairies who represented a tangible threat to humans. There are multiple accounts in the Scottish witchcraft trial records of witches who were taught by the fairies or given fairy familiars by the fairy queen who described the fairies they interacted with as both helpful and also terrifying at times and as beings willing and able to cause the witch harm (Wilby, 2005). The new modern view typified by Conway's work instead depicts the Unseelie in line with what is found in urban fantasy: beings who can be dangerous but ultimately aren't a threat to those who connect to them, whether embodied as the protagonist or the witch, and who act in relatable human ways.

For many people in contemporary America popular culture and fiction form the basis of their knowledge of fairies, rather than traditional folk beliefs. Because of that this evolution of the fairy courts and correlating changes in how fairies themselves are understood is more impactful than it may seem on the surface and directly effects belief. This evolution has also occurred quickly compared to the much slower development within the Scottish system that can be seen previously. What we find is a clear shift in belief, from the source cultures of the fairy faith to modern fiction.

Although often dressed in the trappings of folklore the fairies of modern fiction are not folkloric beings but exist within the confines of the author's plot needs. This in turn heavily impacts the ways that the fairy courts are depicted, beginning with the transition from a locally focused belief into a concept that is universally applied across all fairies so that a story is provided with immediate 'good' and 'bad' sides to both pit against each other and for the protagonist to interact with; this is further complicated by the inbuilt plot twist of having the publicly good group be evil and the publicly bad group be allied with the protagonist, something that has become so common across the last couple decades as to effectively be its own trope now. Yet these fictional fairies and their courts are becoming folklore as the years pass, with more and more people looking to these novels to understand these beings and carrying the ideas from these books forward.

Chapter 7

A Human's Guide to Surviving in a Fairy Court

> *"Elves seldom give unguarded advice, for advice is a dangerous gift, even from the wise to the wise, and all courses may run ill."*
>
> JRR Tolkien, *The Lord of the Rings*

To wrap up this book I'm going to move away from the purely observational and academic material I've focused on thus far and offer readers a different understanding of the fairy courts, a summary of things that have been discussed and advice based on existing fairylore. Think of this as a set of general suggestions and tips for a human who finds themselves interacting with a fairy court and use that as you will, whether it's purely for intellectual interest, towards writing fiction, or towards your own personal use.

> ***Disclaimer**: this advice is meant as a guideline only and no guarantee is offered or implied that following these suggestions will keep your internal organs internal, your form human and not, say, vaguely donkey-shaped (or headed), or protect you from the consequences of an angry fairy monarch/demi-god deciding ensuring your personal misery is their new favourite pastime.*

Before we plunge into court etiquette, we need to first go over some basic general etiquette which applies more generally to the Good Folk. This is something I have said more than once before so if its familiar to you feel free to skip down to the next part where we will get court-specific.

Consider this a bit of a crash course – or the CliffNotes version – in fairy etiquette. Like anything else on this subject for every rule or guideline there's an exception (see my last blog on eating fairy food if you don't understand what I mean by that) but this offers the broad strokes. Before reading this it's important to keep in mind that the Fair Folk in general are not humans and are not like humans; as Yeats would have it, they have few unmixed emotions and are beings of extremes, both good and bad. Often what they do seems perplexing to us, sometimes capricious and sometimes cruel. We cannot approach this subject expecting them to be or do what humans would in any circumstance but we must look at the system they operate in as a guideline to understand their etiquette which is distinct from our own. For example, the Good People have no compunction at all about stealing from humans or harming humans, although we see in folklore that they do have some strict rules about humans doing those same things to them – it is not an equal playing board but one on which they have different sets of rules for themselves and for mortals. This must be understood to understand anything else about them.

This guide, as with the subsequent one on courts, is not so much about the etiquette of fairies among themselves, but of etiquette for humans dealing with fairies. That is a key difference and one to always keep in mind.

Don't lie to the Good People – Fairies are always honest; in folklore and anecdotes they don't lie but always speak the truth. I suspect this is why they can be tricked in ways we perceive as 'easy' sometimes, such as the story where the girl tells the Brownie in the mill her name is 'mise' [myself].[40] As I have mentioned more than once before this does not in any way keep them from tricking us by telling us nothing but the truth in ways that get us to assume a conclusion that is not true. Semantics is an artform of which they are masters. Because they do not lie, they don't expect dishonesty from humans either and as you may imagine they react badly to being lied to. Or, as Briggs succinctly put it: "*The trickiest fairies, like the Devil, were not above equivocation, but they expected strict truth in their dealings with mortals.*" (Briggs, 1976, p 417)

Keep your word – Building off that last one, should you ever be in the position to make a promise or take an oath to a fairy under no circumstances should you break your word. They don't grade on a curve for this one – a promise is a promise and an oath is an oath. Do what you say you will do. This means it is very important not to rashly make promises and to be sure that you only promise things you can fulfil. There are various accounts across folklore of a human making a promise to a fairy and then being held to their word, no matter the circumstances, and equally there are many stories of fairies who promise to do something for a human and fulfil their word, although not always in the way that the human expected.

Lending and borrowing – It happens that the Good Neighbours do sometimes ask the loan of things from us, and it usually wise to give it. This can range from food to grain to items (usually household items or farm equipment). They always repay their debts, most often with interest but not always in kind; for example, there is a well-known anecdote about a man who lent the fairies wheat and was repaid with more than he gave but in barley. There are also stories of fairy mothers who ask a nursing human mother to let a fairy baby nurse just once from them in trade for a blessing; again, this is considered good to do. Humans may also borrow from the Gentry but slightly more caution is required as folklore tells us that a deadline for re-payment is always set and must not be missed. Generally, it is safe to lend out an item as it will be returned in the same condition it was lent, however, there are certain times of year, such as Bealtaine, when it is considered bad luck to lend anything out, especially to one of the Fair Folk, as they will take the luck of the household or person with them. So, this is as is so often the case with these beings a rule that has an exception.

The issue of wash water – This one is a bit complex, but generally speaking, one should not throw dirty water on the ground without an audible warning first, to alert the fairies, and one should not pour such water out over a large rock, lest it be the abode of fairies. Fairies abhor filth and seem to have an especial hatred of dirty water and urine (both of which can be used as protection against them). There is also the matter of having dirty water standing in the home, something that was more common in the past when people would come in and wash their feet; this 'foot water' depending on the area of belief would either drive fairies away or conversely allow them entry into an otherwise protected home.

Gifts – If offered a gift it is wise to accept it and to offer something in return; however, fairy gifts are rarely what they seem. That which seems valuable initially often turns out to be worthless and that which seems like nothing at first is often revealed to be quite valuable. Fairy gifts are also, as often as not, traps, and so great caution should be used with them. In many stories we see something given as a gift that does indeed bring luck or happiness to the person who receives it, but in other cases the item – particularly if it is food or drink – may act to trap the person or bind them to Fairy. Gifts are never straightforward. You really have to use your head here, because accepting them can be a good idea and refusing them can anger the fairies, but sometimes refusing them is the best choice.

Nothing is free – Related to the subjects of lending/borrowing and gifts, try to keep in mind that nothing is free. Even gifts that are given as true gifts without hidden traps still come with obligations. Fairy is a very feudal system in that respect, everything is tied together through debts and obligations and what's owed to who. If you give to them then they owe you in return, even if that owing is paid back simply by not causing you mischief. If they give you gifts then gifts are expected in return. Reciprocity and obligatory return are the foundations of their society, at least in much of folklore and my experience.

Never say thank you – It is a widespread belief, although not ubiquitous, that one shouldn't say thank you to the fairies. I have heard one theory behind this, that it implies a debt to them, a blank check if you will, that would allow them to decide how you repay them. Another theory suggests it is dismissive and implies you feel superior to them. Whatever is the case you should try to avoid saying it. Offering a gift in exchange for something you feel you've received can be a good idea, or saying something else along the lines of expressing gratitude for what happened without saying thank you directly, such as 'I am so happy with —' or 'I really appreciate —'.

Silence – it is possible for a person to have the favour of the Other Crowd and to gain by it. However, the fairies have a strict rule about a person not speaking of experiences or blessing they get from the Good People. I think this is why we have more negative stories than positive and why we have more stories of single encounters than multiple ones. A person can sometimes get permission to speak or to reveal things, but the general rule is that to keep their favour you must stay silent about their activity in your life. Those who brag about fairy blessings or gifts almost always lose them and the future possibility of them.

Privacy – Fairies really, really do not like being spied on or having their privacy invaded. Many stories in folklore involve a person who stumbles across the Good People doing their normal thing, is seen watching, and punished severely – in only a few cases does the person manage to talk their way out of any repercussions. It's a good idea to respect their places and to trust your instincts when you feel like you should or shouldn't go somewhere. If you do happen upon fairies it is probably best to stay quiet and hidden, and wait for them to move on, unless they make it clear from the start they know you are there.

Accept the hypocrisy of it all – one thing that is more universal than anything else may be the idea that fairies have a different set of rules for themselves than for humans. This being the case it is wise to go into fairy etiquette with an understanding that behaviour we see fairies engaging in with each other may not be appropriate for a human to do, or may have very different consequences. Katherine Briggs in her *A Dictionary Of Fairies* relates a story of a trow boy who is cast out from his community for stealing from other trows; even though they regularly steal from humans and that is seen as acceptable they do not tolerate their own people stealing from each other. There are two sets of rules in play, and it's wise to have some idea of which rulebook you are operating from.

This is a quick look at the basics of fairy etiquette, concepts that are found across folk belief and in many stories. As with everything there are exceptions and what is listed here is intentionally very general – specific groups and specific folklore will have different approaches to these things and may have very different rules. This is why I have always encouraged people to look at specific folklore and beliefs around particular beings to help shape a deeper understanding of fairy etiquette, as I am limited by these general ideas because of how contradictory the specifics can be. When in doubt try to go with the most cautious option.

Moving on from basic fairy etiquette we can dig into the etiquette around fairy courts and dealing with the fairy monarchs. These two things are closely connected because if you are actually engaging with a court in the royal sense then you are dealing with those around the monarch or the monarch themselves; if it's a court in the general group of fairies sense, default to the already discussed etiquette. This is the human world equivalent of the difference between daily manners and manners when dealing with an authority figure or someone who significantly socially outranks you, or between every day manners and high society manners. Many of the underlying ideas expressed above hold true but there are also other layers of behaviour to consider. Keep in mind though that every fairy court in each culture is slightly different and these are only general guidelines based mostly on Scottish and Irish Fairy Courts – you'll still need to think on your feet, adapt, and use common sense.

Respect: 'Seelie or Unseelie, offend them and you're doomed'. While some people do hold the view that there are fairies who are utterly safe to deal with, its more widely understood that interacting with the Good Neighbours carries some inherent risk. With the two courts people tend to assume that the Unseelie are dangerous and the Seelie are safe or easier to deal with, but this is a misunderstanding (which hopefully was cleared up in the first few chapters). The Seelie are less likely to take immediate offence and more likely to be somewhat lenient, however, to offend either group will have dire consequences. There are versions of the ballad of *Tam Lin* where the fairy queen is explicitly called the Seelie queen, and after the female protagonist successfully rescues Tam Lin, the queen immediately curses her for daring to steal away one of her folk. In other words, just because the Seelie are *safer* doesn't mean they are *safe*.

What this means in a practical sense is that you want to be respectful no matter which court you are dealing with, and remember that a fairy Queen or King is royalty and should be approached as such. Respect is an easy thing to give to beings who can potentially cause you great harm, and disrespect has a steep price. Keep that in mind. It's also worth always remembering that no matter how connected you think you are or feel like you are to these beings as a human you will always be the lowest social rank – act accordingly.

Proper Manners: pinky up, mouth shut. This one is a bit more nuanced and possibly controversial because, again, there is considerable variance here depending on who and what you are dealing with. That said, however, being polite is never going to be the wrong choice, so it's a safe approach to take. Rather like having good manners in a casual setting may make you look a bit stuffy but won't hurt anything, but having casual manners in a formal setting can cause you problems.

When in doubt, err on the side of formal manners. And silence will always get you further in uncertain situations than running your mouth – unless you are lucky enough that whoever you are dealing with finds you amusing, which does happen. Like I said, nuance. Also, situational awareness goes a long way here and the ability to read a room (while keeping in mind the different rules for fairies and humans).

Part of what makes this controversial is the sheer range of depictions of fairy monarchy and courts we are dealing with. Some are clearly much more formal and reminiscent of human royal courts in their behaviour, while others are quite casual and relaxed – so much so that the royalty may not stand out from the common folk around them. John Kruse discusses this in more depth in his book *How Things Work in Faery* but the short version is that we do have stories of fairy royalty doing very mundane things, including their own laundry. Finnbheara, the fairy king of Galway Ireland, is known in tales to have a fondness for attending horse races and sometimes inviting others who enjoy the sport back to his hall for a meal and in *Thomas of Erceldoune* the fairy queen is first encountered while out hunting alone in the woods. In contrast literary depictions of fairy courts from England and France – especially romances – tend to depict the courts as formal, structured places with a clear delineation between the monarch and their subjects, as can be seen, for example, in the middle Breton lay *Sir Orfeo*.

In short, it's always better to treat a fairy monarch as if they are a monarch, than to treat them casually or as if they are beneath you. You might think that advice is obvious, but trust me it isn't.

Know Your Place: why are you there? Context is everything in these situations and why you are there makes a huge difference in dealing with the fairy courts.

Are you an invited guest? If so, by whom? Did you arrive on your own? Are you there for a purpose or did you just wander in? Is the encounter an accident? Each of these possible scenarios puts you in a different position while you are visiting a fairy court, in the same way that you approaching a fairy queen is profoundly different that a queen approaching you. In most of the cultures that we find fairy beliefs in historically there was a strong emphasis on hospitality and guest rights, which carries over to fairy courts and belief where being a guest is much safer than being an interloper – although being a guest has some downsides as well because it carries reciprocal obligations. If this sounds complicated it's because it is, but it's also important. Keep in mind why you are interacting with the court or monarch and how that shapes those interactions, what you and they are obligated to do or not do, and how friendly they may be – which will be very different if you are visiting on the Queen's invitation versus invading to try to rescue a stolen human, for example.

Know Your Role: who are you to them? Related to the last point – the other side of that coin if you will – is that it's important to know who you are to the beings you are encountering. This context throughout folklore and modern anecdotes matters a great deal. Are you a stranger who is trying to establish a connection? Then act like that and expect to be treated like that. Are they trying to recruit you to some purpose? We find that in many of the Scottish witchcraft trial accounts, where an accused witch would describe being approached by the fairies or fairy queen in order to serve them in some capacity. Are you a lover or potential lover? That's another thing we see in many stories, and while it still puts all the control on the fairy end of the relationship it puts you in a different position than an acquaintance or servant or friend/ally. Basically, how do you fit in to their social structure? Courts, as we've discussed, are very rigid, hierarchical dynamics and how you fit into that hierarchy matters; and trust me as a human you aren't at the top.

It is probably worth saying here that when engaging with these beings – unless you are using this material as a guide to writing fiction, but even then – don't fall into the trap of believing you are the main character of the story. Main characters in stories – besides not existing in our tangible reality – have lovely things like plot armour[41] and dues ex machina[42] on their side. Don't put yourself into a foolish, dangerous situation because you think nothing bad can or will happen to you. Anthropocentricism is not your friend in a fairy court.

Patronage is a double-edged blade. It is very common across older accounts and in some modern accounts for a human to be interacting with a fairy court or monarch because they are in service to the fairies in some context; this can include witches who have sworn allegiance to a fairy queen or king, humans who are being taught by the fairies (music and esoteric skills being the most common things fairies might teach a human), or because the human has a fairy lover. In these cases, the fairy or fairy monarch the person is connected to would in effect be their patron among the fairies. The human owes this fairy loyalty in some implicit or explicit context and the fairy in turn offers protection, luck, and usually some knowledge. Thomas the Rhymer served the Fairy Queen and was under her protection while in Fairy, as well as being paid with the gift of 'true speech' after he left. Elph Irving in the *Faerie Oak of Corriewater* was taken into the Fairy Queens service and paid with a kiss.[43] Scottish witch Bessie Dunlop was paid in *'goods and gear'*, Isobel Gowdie was given fine food and magical skill, and Andro Mann was both the Fairy queen's lover and taught by her how to be a cunningman. In every case we look at we find some sort of exchange, where the human pledges loyalty, temporarily or permanently, and the fairies/fairy monarch pays them in some way for that service. On the surface this can look very appealing, and aspects of it certainly are, however, it should be kept in mind that this patronage has an additional cost, beyond whatever is agreed to.[44] Whether we are talking about the Scottish courts with their clashing agendas towards humans or the Irish courts and their clashing agendas towards each other, or any other fairy court for that matter, we are talking about groups which by nature have internal and external allies and enemies just as a human royal court would. When you come in and ally with a specific fairy or fairy group you are taking on those allies and enemies as well.

Despite what some people might like to think about themselves if you have a specific patronage in Fairy, with very few exceptions, you are not a neutral party any longer. Let me give you a story as an example. There is an account relayed by WB Yeats about a man who was asked by two rival groups of fairies to referee a competitive game they were playing, which, of course, was far more crucial than a mere game. The group who won praised the man and promised him good luck and fortune; the group who lost, however, swore they would have their revenge. Three years later when the man was out walking alone the rival fairy group gave him the 'fairy touch' which rendered him insane from that day forward. Siding with one group meant making an enemy of the other. If you are connected to or allied with a group that has known animosity or rivalries with others then you are now part of that as well, whether you choose to be or not. Consider this carefully.

Every Promise is a weapon, it's up to you to wield it or be cut by it. I mentioned in the first section under 'keep your word' the importance of promises in Fairy and why its unwise to make them and essential to keep them. When it comes to promises specifically in a fairy court or to a fairy monarch this is even more important because a promise is often a method of control and sometimes a test of loyalty. If you are asked for a promise you don't need to make it, but refusing often has a price – so choose wisely. Also be very careful how you word any promises to cover yourself as much as possible. It is possible to use oaths and promises to your own advantage – we see this with the story of Sir Orfeo. Orfeo is able to successfully rescue his wife, who was stolen by the fairy king, because he has entered the court in the guise of a musician and the king has promised to reward his skill with any boon he would ask for; Orfeo requests his wife be given back to him. When the fairy king initially refuses, claiming that the woman is too good for him, Orfeo reminds him of his promise and points out that it is worse to break a promise, to be foresworn, than to give what Orfeo is asking. The king relents rather than break his word. In contrast if you make a promise expect to be held to it in whatever way will be least advantageous to you. It is very rare for a human who breaks a promise to a fairy to be forgiven for it, and usually the consequences are severe. In one Scottish account a woman's fairy lover made her swear never to reveal his presence and when she did so (by telling her sister about him) he left her forever which drove her mad (Briggs, 1976). When the fairy Pressine's husband broke his promise not to see her when she is giving birth or bathing their children she is forced to leave with their daughters, and when her daughter Melusine's husband breaks his promise not to see her on Saturdays she is transformed into a half-serpent and forced to leave. Promises have power and consequences. Be clever in how and what you promise, and always view a promise as a blade. You can use it to your own advantage if you are smart and careful, but you can also hurt yourself with it if you aren't.

Monarchs have different rules except when they don't – perhaps the most difficult thing about this subject is that all rules and guidelines are actually fluid and flexible. This is true for fairies in general but even more so for the queens and kings. For example, it is usually not advised to accept or eat fairy food or drink, as it will act to trap you in Fairy, but these same things offered by a fairy monarch are safe to accept and consume, and we have various stories of people doing so without any negative consequence. It is extremely unwise to refuse a gift offered by a monarch, even when accepting it is obviously a bad thing for you. To refuse something offered by a monarch is to insult them, but to accept it is to accept the cost that comes with it. As we discussed above nothing is free and that remains true for the Rulers of Fairy, although sometimes the cost that comes with their gifts is more subtle. We do have a range of stories of humans who were entertained by a fairy queen or king and walked away relatively unscathed; Finnbheara, for example, was known to invite humans to feast with his people and Áine has been seen dancing with human revellers on her hill, without any harm to the humans involved. But on the same hand when the fairy queen offered Scottish witch Bessie Dunlop '*goods and gear*' it was in exchange for Bessie swearing fealty to her above all others and Isobel Gowdie was given good food by the Fairy Queen but was made to use elf-shot against other humans. It is also no simple matter to refuse a monarch of Fairy. Thomas the Rhymer served the Fairy Queen for seven years and was given the gift of '*a tongue that never lied*', a gift he initially tried to refuse as he knew that speaking only truth would make his life in the human world difficult, but the fairy queen would brook no argument and at her insistence he eventually accepted.

Landless Feudalism: when the people are the country. I have often compared fairy social structure to feudalism, and that is useful but also perhaps a bit misleading. I use the term because it's the best I know of to describe a culture that is held together by a rigid hierarchy dependant on complex webs of allegiance and interdependence. In true feudalism the basis for everything is land ownership and land rights, but this isn't so for Fairy where the country is less a place and more the group of affiliated people. Although an argument can be made for the land of Fairy as well as fairies being territorial over human places, the social system doesn't seem to be based on land ownership in the way human feudalism is. What we find instead is various references to belonging to specific groups and often to kings or queens, as well as a wider social structure that mimics, at least externally, the feudalism of Europe in the middle ages. The fairy monarch us ultimately the most powerful person, with various other beings who owe them fealty and in turn others who serve; we have references to everything from queens and nobility to knights, to basic servants and farmhands. In the 21st century this structure is vastly different than what we find in the human world, even places that still have monarchies, and may offer a bit of culture shock to humans interacting with it. The world of Fairy does evolve but thus far it doesn't seem to have grown beyond this social structure. This is important to keep in mind when dealing with a fairy court if you want to avoid offending anyone there.

What will you give? A key question to ask yourself as you engage with a court or monarch is what exactly you are willing to give. They will ask – maybe sooner maybe later – for something from you and if you want to be able to negotiate for yourself (and trust me you do) then you need to have some idea of where your own personal limits are. Please understand these requests won't be symbolic no matter how much they are couched in metaphor or allusion. Tears, for example, usually represent feelings or in some story's memories. Hair and blood represent the physical body. To give these things is to give at least a small part of yourself. Names have power, so to give a name that you feel strongly connected to or emotionally invested in is to give access to that part of yourself. The poem *Goblin Market* illustrates this idea fairly well, with a character trading a piece of her hair for goblin fruit, only to realize she's traded away her mortal life.

- Do not go into these situations thinking you are the smartest person in the room and assuming you can easily make deals. Go into things with a firm boundary on what you are willing to give, which includes your time and effort as well as actual physical things. It also includes your self.

- Once something is given, once a deal is made, you will be bound to it. There are no take-back-sies when it comes to fairies, at least not without a considerable fight, and it doesn't matter whether you understood what you were giving up or not.

What won't you give? As with so many things fairy there are two sides to the what will you give coin, and the flip side is what won't you give? You must understand what your own limits are, both in the sense of what you are actually able to do or not do and what you will not trade away. This is important for several reasons: firstly, because if you don't have any limits, they will inevitably consume you. Possibly literally. Secondly because if you offer what isn't yours to give or what you cannot actually do then you are, effectively, breaking a promise and there will be consequences. Thirdly though, and perhaps most importantly, if they want what you offer, they will take it whether or not you actually want to give it. You can't just change your mind when you realize this is serious, and I have seen and heard stories of people deeply regretting giving something they don't actually want to lose. For example, when Bessie Dunlop made a deal with the fairy queen in 17th century Scotland her baby died. Don't give what you can't bear to lose and don't let the fairies set the price.

- It is best to approach dealing with the fairy courts very seriously and to assume that things will have consequences. Treating them as a joke because popculture tends to portray fairies as children's fantasy can lead to trouble. There is a story that goes around in New England about a pagan midsummer event in the early 21st century which was dedicated to the fairies, wherein people were able to come up to the altar and make offerings. One man walked up with his child and offered her, much to the horror of the people gathered around. He thought it was funny because to him fairies were silly, but to those around him who knew that fairies had a long-held reputation for stealing human children his actions were extremely inappropriate and also dangerous. Don't be this guy.

Know your limits and stick to them, no matter what.

Be nice or be ruthless. There are two ways to approach interacting with a fairy court: you can be nice or you can be ruthless. Each has advantages and each has a cost. Nice means exactly what is sounds like, act in ways that are pleasant and considerate, be agreeable; be kind to those around you and try to engage from a place of amity. The advantage here is that being nice is much better for making allies across a range of people in court. It can also put you into a slightly safer place to start. We have many stories of people who succeed in fairy because they extend kindness to the beings around them. The disadvantage here is, of course, the flip side to that; being nice can make you look vulnerable or weak and can make you a target especially in a fairy court where "cut throat" isn't just an expression. Whether this is a weakness or a strength depends entirely on you. In contrast you can choose to be ruthless, an especially wise choice if you are there for a specific purpose which is against the fairies' desires or goals. If you want to rescue a stolen human, for example, your odds are better with ruthlessness than niceness. Ruthlessness puts you in a position of more control and more power, but it also requires a very strong will and unwavering commitment to your goals. It is a salting-the-earth approach. The obvious disadvantage, besides the need to fully commit to it, is that it can earn you the enmity of the fairies who have very, very long memories and a creative sense of revenge.

In Sir Orfeo the protagonist rescues his wife by entering the fairy king's hall and entertaining him as a musician until he is offered a reward. In *Childe Rowland* the protagonist succeeds in rescuing his sister where his brothers failed because he is utterly ruthless and (as instructed before entering Fairy) he beheads anyone who speaks to him, no matter how helpful they have been, and ultimately his sister as well for speaking – which frees his real sister and his brothers from the Fairy King's enchantment. In a folk story from Galway a man successfully saves his bride from the Fairy King, Finnbheara, who has kidnapped her, by digging into the sidhe, the fairy mound, and salting[45] the earth which forces the fairies to return her. Orfeo takes the nice approach and it works for him, partially because he happens to also be a skilled musician. Childe Rowland and the man in Galway take the ruthless approach and are successful at least in the short term, although they certainly earn some fairy enemies for their efforts.

In a fairy court you must anticipate all the politicking, intrigue, drama, plots, and backstabbing – figurative and literal – you'd expect in a human royal court but to an extreme degree. These are beings with millennia to hold a grudge or nurture a secret romance, to jockey for social positions or plot against others; they have more time than a human can truly comprehend to spend on their games. A human pushing into that crowd needs a strategy and an understanding of what they are stepping into.

Nice is the baseline I recommend people start from because you can go from nice to ruthless but you cannot go from ruthless to nice – once that bridge is burned it is well and truly dust and ash.

Trust no one, not even yourself. Fairy is a land of illusion and magic, and the fairy courts are places of intrigue and danger. Normally my advice to people engaging with fairies is to be careful who you trust and to vet allies and spirits as much as possible, but this gets a bit more complicated with fairy courts and fairy monarchs. It would be a bad idea to be openly sceptical of a Fairy Queen but it would also be a bad idea to fully trust any being of Fairy, including a Queen. Trust is a gift that should be earned and it is something that makes a human vulnerable in many ways. On the same hand being open with your lack of trust is also dangerous. You need to be canny here and choose who you give your trust to and how far that trust extends. Often enough those who seem the most helpful are the least trustworthy and under no circumstances should you use physical appearance as a guide for this because in Fairy that which is most appealing in appearance is often a baited trap, and because of the power and impact of illusion things may not be anything like they look. That second part is also why you can't even trust yourself fully. Your own sense will be used against you and your reflexive trust of what you see, hear, and touch will become a weapon to manipulate you. If this seems overly cynical or pessimistic then you need to familiarize yourself more with older folklore and modern anecdotes, because this is actually the gentle version.

This advice not only goes for interactions you may have with fairy courts, etc., but also for any knowledge or information you are given I these encounters. Double check everything, verify as much as you can – never simply take something at face value because its coming from a fairy source. Many times, the information can be fact checked and will prove true, but keep in mind the way that fairies approach telling the truth and semantics – it's entirely possible for them to tell you something that is both true and misleading. There's a saying "every mushroom is edible but some are only edible once"[46] which can be a good example here: if someone tells you all mushrooms can be eaten, they aren't lying but they are intentionally leaving out vital information the lack of which will result in harm. Fairies are often like this, fairy monarchs inclusive. They have no motivation to provide you all the necessary context and, in many cases, find it entertaining to intentionally not do so. Trust nothing, question everything.

Guard your heart. This is necessary on both a physical and emotional level. Humans are on the menu in Fairy and you can't ever let yourself forget that, but there's more ways that a person can lose themselves to a fairy court than being hunted for sport.

So, rule one is don't agree to anything involving your body that could potentially mean physical harm unless you feel very confident that you understand the risks and consequences. We have many accounts of various kinds of fairies eating humans, including at least one from Lady Wilde where fairies made a feast out of an old woman's corpse, so its unwise to ever think this isn't a possibility. It's also vital to understand that the fairies' concept of consent and the human concept of consent are not the same concepts. For one thing consent with fairies can't be revoked, only renegotiated. For another fairies consider consent given under extreme duress valid; Elspeth Roech was kept awake for days and harassed by a fairy man until she agreed to have sex with him.

Rule two is, as much as possible, try to guard your emotions. It is easy to fall in love with Fairy and with individual fairies, and while there are accounts where that ends well there are just as many where it ends very badly. It is *possible* for a fairy to genuinely love a human as we seem to see in the story of Sir Lanaval where even after breaking his word not to speak of his fairy lover she still returns to defend him and ultimately takes him back to Fairy with her or as we see in an Irish story related by Lady Wilde where a man is taken into the fairy hill by his lover and refuses to be rescued when his family attempts it because he prefers to stay with her. Or, if we are counting kelpies as fairies, there is the story of the kelpie who loves a human so much that he allows himself to bound by a magical bridle for a year in order to become human and marry her. But for every story with a happy ending we find more stories where the human breaks a promise and is abandoned forever or finds themselves trapped when their love fails and the fairy's doesn't. Evens-Wentz relates the story of a man with a fairy lover who grew too overbearing; the man tried to flee to Canada to escape her only to have her follow him. It is also wise to keep in mind that a human's love may not be returned in kind and that love can also be a weapon used against you, even if the fairy tells you that they love you – because words are twisty things and love has many layers of meaning. You might love them romantically and they might love you the way a human would love a pretty sunset or pet hamster. Emotions influence us into forgetting all the common sense and all the fairy etiquette we know and convince us that we are the exception to every rule. So, when possible, try to be careful where your love is going and at the least be aware of how it is being used. People will do things for love they would never otherwise do.

There are other points that can be added to this list but we start to get into nuances and rules of specific groups, so I'll stop here. The things we've covered are enough at least to keep a human reasonably safe – or as safe as is possible – when interacting with a fairy court or monarch. I'll end this by saying that every rule has an exception so don't approach this advice as anything more than that. In the end there's an unpredictability to these things, even in stories, that can't be overcome.

Conclusion

"Some fairy lore makes a clear division between good and wicked types of fairies — between those who are friendly to mankind, and those who seek to cause us harm. In Scottish tales, good fairies make up the Seelie Court, which means the Blessed Court, while bad fairies congregate in the Unseelie Court... Yet in other traditions, a fairy can be good or bad, depending on the circumstance or on the fairy's whim. They are often portrayed as amoral beings, rather than as immoral ones, who simply have little comprehension of human notions of right and wrong."

Terri Windling, *The Faery Reel: Tales from the Twilight Realm*

The fairy courts are a popular subject today, rising from an obscure position in local Scottish folklore to prominence in urban fantasy and role-playing games, where the simple idea of two rival, morally opposed, groups of fairies has been expanded and elaborated on to create a complex social system. What many people who know the modern systems may not realize is the complicated backstory behind the current iterations, and hopefully this book has helped clarify both what the courts are and how they have evolved over the last 400 years.

I am, of course, in no way trying to tell anyone what to believe or what they should believe and there are now a wide range of understandings built up around these concepts. But I think it's important to explore the history and to appreciate that the older views still exist as lived belief in many places. The new hasn't subsumed the old, at least not yet and not fully, but rather these layers of belief exist side by side across communities. To some people the Seelie and Unseelie are still as they have been for the last two hundred years in Scottish folklore, a way to understand fairies as either inclined to help humans or to hurt them. For others the courts exist as they have been developed across role-playing games, especially *Changeling,* and rather than moral implications between groups we find the tension between tradition and innovation, between selflessness and selfishness. For yet others the Seelie and Unseelie are understood via fiction and may fit into a range of possibilities from an extreme, distilled version of good and bad morality to an absolute role reversal where the Seelie are the danger and the Unseelie the saviour. Modern anecdotes – encounters relayed by people today – include this entire spectrum of possibility.

Have the courts actually changed and evolved? Are they different in the 21st century than the 18th or 19th? This is a question that has as many answers as we have stories. Certainly, belief in them has changed, has spread, has been widely applied, and they have been renamed, but even through all of that the core concepts have been consistent. The idea that the fairies exist in groupings which have different relationships towards humans remains in belief, in fiction, in gaming, in all the ways that humans interact with the concept of fairies. And yet as universal as the idea can feel and is often portrayed, it has never actually been universal and it still isn't. It spreads like ink in water, further every year, but besides Scottish folk belief – specifically lowland Scottish folk belief – its stronghold is fiction. It is still largely foreign to Irish or Welsh folklore, and certainly more so further afield, and yet fiction is a powerful vehicle of belief. Already the ideas are being incorporated into some aspects of pagan spirituality and included in active belief by those who are building their understanding of fairies with fiction as a foundation instead of existing folklore. And so, like everything related to the subject of fairies, the waters become muddy and the more we seek the less certainty we find. The fairy courts are only Scottish folk belief, except where they aren't. The Seelie are helpful and the Unseelie hurtful, except where that is reversed. Belief is a fluid thing which changes and reshapes itself and in places where this belief is untethered from cultural support it has been shaped in radically new ways that build using the trappings of the old to cover the innovation underneath.

There is something about the idea of the two courts that seems to appeal to many people on a deep level. Perhaps it is the simplicity of an us or them structure, perhaps it's the neatness of having a being's intentions made clear by this system of alignment, or perhaps it's an inborn desire for the world to be either good or bad by nature regardless of our own actions. The newer views of the fairy courts are often overly simplified and in turn flatten the human responsibility as well, especially those that render the Unseelie into misunderstood good guys who only need the right person to relate to them. But when we go back to the original Scottish beliefs, we see that fairies have always been complex, always represented both risk and reward, and that even the good ones were dangerous if offended. All of the responsibility for the outcomes of interactions rested on the human in the equation and whether or not they were polite enough, canny enough, and cautious enough.

Appendix A

Glossary

In this appendix I'm going to offer a short list of some basic terms used throughout the book which readers may find helpful.

Anthropocentricism – Assuming that humans are the centre of everything and always the most important in any situation. As applied to fairies also assuming humans hold all the power in any interaction.

Anthropomorphism – Applying or assuming human characteristics or traits onto a non-human person, thing, etc.

Aos sidhe – The people of the fairy hills.

Autumn Court – In some newer systems the courts are divided into four rather than two, based on the seasons of the year. Autumn is usually considered a subgroup of Winter (the Unseelie) or allied with them.

Bright court – An alternate name for the seelie court found in urban fantasy.

Changeling – (1) The name of a popular role-playing game. (2) A term found across fairy belief for an item, aged fairy, or sickly fairy baby that is exchanged via deception for a healthy human who in turn is stolen into the world of Fairy.

Court – Two main meanings: a monarch and those who serve them, or in Scots also a group.

Dark court – An alternate name for the unseelie used in some urban fantasy.

Elf – A humanoid supernatural being that strongly resembles a human but has magical powers and superior skills, especially in music and crafting.

Fae – An old French word for a being with supernatural or enchanting powers. Used in some modern contexts for any and all beings of the Otherworld.

Faery/Faerie – Variant spelling of fairy.

Fairy – A catch all term used since the 1300s for a being of the Otherworld or world of Fairy. In some modern contexts it is used specifically and only for small twee winged sprites.

Fall court – See autumn court.

Folklore – The beliefs, traditions, or practices of a group of people.

Folkloresque – A term used in folklore studies to indicate something that draws on or is inspired by folklore but isn't folklore itself.

LARP – Live action role-playing. A game which is physically acted out as its played.

Otherkin – People who believe they are either a non-human soul in a human body or that they have non-human ancestry.

RPG – Role-playing game.

Seelie – Blessed, lucky, fortunate.

Seelie court – In Scottish folk belief a group of fairies who are more kindly inclined towards humans.

Sidhe – Shee – literally meaning fairy hill or fairy mound but often used as a slang term for the beings who inhabit such places.

Sìth – Shee – the Scottish Gaidhlig of the Irish sidhe, with the same general meaning.

Slua or Sluagh – A word meaning host, assembly, or army. The Slua Sidhe are a malicious group of sidhe who travel through the air and cause harm.

Spring court – In some newer systems, that use four courts instead of two, spring is either a subgroup of Summer (seelie) or allied with it.

Summer court – A newer label for the Seelie court which tries to avoid moral implications by relating the courts to seasons. It is worth noting, however, that summer is still given the more positive qualities.

TTRPG – Table top role-playing game. A game that is played around a table where the action is narrated by the players.

Unseelie – Unlucky, ungodly.

Unseelie court – In Scottish folklore a group of fairies who are malicious towards humans without any provocation. Includes various beings who are predatory towards humans.

Wight – A Scots word for any being.

Winter court – A newer way to understand the Unseelie court which tries to avoid moral implications by tying the court to a season. It is worth noting that winter is still given the more negative, dangerous qualities.

Wyldfae – A term coined by Jim Butcher and used for the third group of fairies who don't belong to either court.

Appendix B

Recommended Resources

At this point there aren't that many accessible sources on the Scottish Fairy Courts, in part because the early modern material casts a broader net which often misses the seelie court, in part because the unseelie court as a concept is relatively new – only about 200 years old – and in part because no one seems to be looking too closely at 20th and 21st century beliefs around these subjects. Most of the books I would normally recommend on Scottish fairy belief don't mention the courts, including the work of Rev. Robert Kirk which is some of the earliest and most fascinating to look at. A person who is interested in learning more will have little choice but to carefully work through as much source material as possible to piece together what evidence we have, as I have done here – in fact a large part of why I wrote this book was to try to offer the best resource I could for people researching the fairy courts.

For nonfiction sources on this aspect of Scottish folk belief, I can only suggest two sources. F. Marian McNeill's *Silver Bough* volume 1 is an option and I recommend the work of Lizanne Henderson as well, although both only tangentially touch on the courts.

Beyond the scanty nonfiction sources, I'd like to include a small list of various novels which include or primarily feature the traditional fairy courts. I'll discuss a little about each book, why I recommend it, and how closely – or not – it adheres to older ideas about the fairy courts. Obviously, this isn't an exhaustive list, but it highlights the books I think people might enjoy and which also incorporate more folklore into their fiction than others might.

Top Recommendations

These are the main books that I suggest people look for if they want good folkloric depictions of fairies and the fairy courts in modern stories. No book is going to be 100% perfect but these are as close as I can think of, and they are also good stories.

War For the Oaks by Emma Bull tells the story of a human musician in Minneapolis who is unwillingly pulled into a conflict between the seelie and unseelie courts because they require a human participant to engage in war. Well written and with interesting characters, the story has properly ruthless fairies and a good basis in folklore.

Faery Sworn by Ron C Neito is a very creative story but overall, fairly true to the folklore. Some variance on what the Seelie and Unseelie courts are called, but does a great job of including things like aversion to iron, viciousness, time slip between Fairy and Earth, and etiquette. My only critique would be at the idea that there are only single beings in some of the categories we know from folklore, ie 'the kelpie' 'the nucklevee', but that's a fairly minor quibble.

The Knowing by Kevin Manwaring is an excellent blend of older fairylore and the modern world. Based on the story of Rev. Robert Kirk but imagining his descendants into our time, very accurate to older fairylore.

Secondary Recommendations

These are also good books; however, they do venture further from the folklore and need to be read with a grain of salt.

Modern Faery Tale series by Holly Black – gets points for portraying fairies along mostly traditional lines, and as ruthless and often cruel; loses points for tons of YA tropes and some major plot holes. The two fairy courts, however, are largely in line with the older ideas about them.

Merry Gentry series by Laurell K Hamilton leans more into erotica than most others discussed here, the series focuses a great deal on the two fairy courts, which in the world of Merry Gentry have established themselves in the United States. Hamilton, however, has a unique approach to the courts, making the Unseelie brutal but ultimately more honest, and the Seelie beautiful in the surface but duplicitous and rotten underneath.

The SERRAted Edge series and ***Bedlam Bard*** series by Mercedes Lackey – Primarily written in the 90's the *SERRAted Edge* series looks at the aos sidhe in modern America and includes a lot of folklore as well as some creative innovation, like the elves reacting to caffeine as if it were an addictive drug. The series is a bit dated at this point. The related *Bedlam Bard* series, which is set in the same universe and has some crossover, is also decent.

Toby Daye series by Seanan McGuire – feature modern fairies in America, reasonably close to folklore in many respects especially as regards politics in Fairy.

So, there you have it. That covers my main recommendations and some secondary recommendations. Generally speaking, I think most urban fantasy, while my favourite genre, tends to fall into the secondary recommendations (I'd even include my own in that by the way) because, in order to create the story, liberties with the folklore have to be taken, especially where there are romantic themes or subthemes which is almost the entire genre. It's often a safe bet to say if the fairies or a fairy in the book are main characters and even slightly relatable or sympathetic then liberties are being taken with the folklore (*Faery Sworn* is a notable and unusual exception).

Endnotes

1. I am using these spellings, but there is a wide array of variation.
2. *The night, the night is Halloween*
   Our seelie court must ride
   Through England and through Ireland both
   And all the world wide
3. The section on courts has been revised and adapted from the entry of the same name in my book *A New Dictionary of Fairies* as has the material in the following chapter on the Scottish courts
4. Courtiers are almost a topic unto themselves to be honest. A courtier was a person who attended the ruler at court and could include members of the nobility, servants, secretaries, merchants, soldiers, clergy, friends of the ruler, lovers, and entertainers. They may or may not hold actual rank in the court depending on a variety of factors. What defined someone as a courtier was the amount of time they spent hanging around the royal court, whether or not they ever actually even interacted with the ruler.
5. *one woman of the Queen of Fairies*
   that will take goods to Fairyland
   through all broad Scotland she has been
   on horseback on Halloween
   and always in seeking certain nights
   as she says, with our Seelie wights
6. The king of Fairy and his court, with the elf Queen; with many elvish incubi were riding that night.
7. *He that tills the fairy green*
   No luck again shall have
   And he that spoils the fairy ring
   Befalls him want and woe

For fortuneless days and weary nights
Are his until his dying day

8. The Queen of Elfland's Nurse.
9. This material is expanded and adapted from my 2024 Romancing the Gothic 'Devils and Justified Sinners' conference presentation 'Tenants of Hell: Fairies, the Devil, and Folk Belief in Early Modern Scotland'.

10. *In the morning, the foul fiend of Hell,*
Among this folk will fetch his fee;
And you are very strong and pleasant,
I well believe he would choose you

11. Wicht or wight is a general term in Scots that means both any living being as well as any supernatural being.
12. It must be noted here for clarity that there is a work of fiction by John Matthews *The Secret Lives of Elves & Fairies* which purports to be the secret personal journal of Rev. Kirk and does use the terms Seelie and Unseelie, but this is a 21st century book, effectively a fantasy novel, and the terms are anachronistic. Unseelie in particular wasn't in common use applied to fairies until around two hundred years after Kirk's lifetime. Reverend Kirk's actual book is called *The Secret Commonwealth of Elves, Fauns, and Fairies*.

13. *If you call me imp or elf*
I counsel you, look well to yourself;
If you call me fairy
I'll work you great misery;
If good neighbor you call me
Then good neighbor I will be;
But if you call me seelie wight
I'll be your friend both day and night

14. *one woman of the Queen of Fairies*
that will take goods to Fairyland
through all broad Scotland she has been

on horseback on Halloween
and always in seeking certain nights
as she says, with our Seelie wights

15. Although I believe in recent decades the idea of the two courts has spread to Ireland, it isn't found in older material to my knowledge and I was unable to find a single reference to the two courts in any of my Irish folklore books. The Irish system is based on a multitude of sidhe (fairy hills) ruled by different kings and queens, with each being its own kingdom in a way. All the Irish Fair Folk, it seems, are ambivalent in nature and cannot easily be placed into a grouping of 'good' or 'wicked'.
16. The blatant misogyny here is typical of 19th century works.
17. King James ruled as James VI in Scotland and James I in England.
18. *"There were a King and Queene of Fairy of such a jolly court & train as they had, how they had a tithe, & duty, as it were, of all goods: how they naturally rode and went, ate and drank, and did all other actions like natural men and women."* The reference to a 'tithe and duty' is to the belief that the fairies were entitled to a portion of human harvests, including milk from cattle, and that this percentage was owed to them by all.
19. *Nicnevin with her nymphs, in number enough*
    With charms from Caithness and the Canonry of Ross
    Whose knowledge consists in casting a ball of yarn...
    The King of Fairy, and his Court, with the Elf Queen,
    with many elvish Incubi was riding that night
20. *"That fourth kind of spirit, which by the Gentiles was called Diana, and her wandering court, and amongst us was called the Fairy (as I told you) or our good neighbours."*
21. While he is more properly known as archangel Michael he has long been referred to as 'saint' Michael across folk practice. That usage will be maintained here.

22. Although she later frees Thomas so that he won't be taken to Hell in the fairies' tithe, somewhat calling this disavowal into question.
23. I must clarify for readers that this description is unclear as to whether it meant a man with black skin or a man with black hair.
24. We will be diving deeply into the influence of fiction on the fairy courts in the following chapters.
25. The Morrigan is not understood or named as a Fairy Queen in any sources or folklore, but is mentioned here as one of the Tuatha De Danann associated with a location that is understood as a sidhe. The sidhe of Cruachan is said to be ruled by Ochall Oichni but it also referred to, under the name Uaimh na gCat, as "the Morrigan's fit abode".
26. A class of people distinct from poets or musicians this would include jugglers, acrobats, dancers and the like.
27. Meaning that ultimately this name isn't a name at all, but merely another title but one that has been absorbed across languages in a way that has caused it to be confused for a name today.
28. Contrary to popular claims, Shakespeare's Mab has no connection to the Irish Medb (Meave). Although the words may look somewhat alike, they sound very different, and mab was a term in use in Shakespeare's time for a lazy or unkempt woman. This may have been his source or alternately he may have been leaning into a version of the name Habundia, but this is uncertain.
29. This should more properly be headed as Germanic but I am trying to avoid confusion and have found too many people think Germanic means German rather than indicating cultures which share a Germanic language.
30. It should be noted here that the term 'sidhe' is often co-opted outside Ireland and used in a sense outside the Irish meaning, and should therefore be understood as distinct

from the Irish term and folklore. In the case of New Age material sidhe is often applied to beings who are incorporeal, all wise or more advanced than humans, and who claim to share a root ancestry with humans that long ago diverged. See both Matthews and Spangler.

31. White Wolf may best be known for their two most popular games: *Vampire the Masquerade*, which even had a brief television showed based off of it, and *Werewolf: the Apocalypse*.
32. This section is written based on my own personal experiences with TTRPGs and LARPs since the late 1990s. Any errors here are entirely my own.
33. Interesting sidenote here, while the words fae and fey were not originally synonymous they have been used as synonyms for the last few decades. Historically fae (which is the root of fairy) is derived from the French and ultimately from Latin, indicating a spirit connected to fate, while fey is derived from Germanic languages and was used, including in Scots, to indicate a person or thing doomed to die. Both are now used in some places as a general term for beings of Fairy or with an Otherworldly nature.
34. Otherkin are people who believe they have non-human souls or non-human ancestry of various types. The folklore behind these ideas goes back hundreds of years and the modern iteration and community as such began to have a public presence by the 1960s and 70s.
35. These observations are casual ones from my own experiences across a range of demographics.
36. While the terms fae and fairy are synonymous, with fae as the old French predecessor of the modern English word fairy, it has become popular in the last decade or so, particularly in urban fantasy, for the term fae to take the place of the general catchall fairy while fairy is given a more specific definition. For my purposes here I will continue to use the

word fairy, but wanted to acknowledge the complex and changing usage found today.

37. In later books in the series this would be expanded to include Scottish and Welsh elves as well, although all are treated as rather homogeneous.
38. There is no deity by that name as far as I have been able to find, but the name is close to that of Andraste, the war goddess worshipped by Queen Boudicca in what is now England.
39. The main ones' people named were Butcher's *Dresden Files* and Black's work, with Hamilton's *Merry Gentry* a somewhat distant third.
40. This, of course, is key to her escape from his vengeful mother after she kills him, because when asked for the name of his attacker he can only repeat 'myself, myself'.
41. Plot armour is the idea that significant or important characters have a degree of safety in a story because they are necessary to the plot.
42. Dues ex machina, god from the machine, is a plot device where an extremely unlikely event occurs to bring a resolution to a story that is happier than should be possible or to solve a seemingly impossible situation.
43. The implication in the poem is that his payment was being her lover.
44. Related side note to this: always read the fine print, and always negotiate on your own behalf or you may very well end up giving far more than you get in return.
45. In some Irish folklore the fairy folk are averse to salt. Salt also ruins the soil it is put into and will prevent anything from growing there.
46. Because eating them will kill you.

Bibliography

Acland, A., (2018) Tam Lin 39 G retrieved from tam-lin.org

Ashif (2024) The Seelie Court in Dungeons and Dragons: A Complete Guide. Retrieved from https://birminghaminsider.co.uk/seelie-dnd/

Barry, G., (1867) *A History of the Orkney Islands*

Black, G., (1894) *Scottish Charms and Amulets*

Black, H., (2002) *Tithe*

Briggs, K., (1967) *The Fairies in Tradition and Literature*

— (1976). *A Dictionary of Fairies*

Brock, M., and Raiswell, R., (2018) *Knowing Demons, Knowing Spirits in the Early Modern Period*

Brosius, M., (2007). *The Court and Court Society in Ancient Monarchies*

Brucato, P., (1996) *Changeling Players Guide*

Bull, E., (1987) *War for the Oaks*

Butcher, J., (2002) *Summer Knight*

— (2010) *Changes*

— (2012) *Cold Days*

Campbell, J., (1900) *The Gaelic Otherworld*

Carmichael, A., (1900) *Carmina Gadelica*

C&MH (2014) Castle Life: Officers and Servants in a Medieval Castle retrieved from http://www.castlesandmanorhouses.com/life_02_officers.htm

Chambers, R., (1842) *Popular Rhymes, Fireside Stories, and Amusements of Scotland*

Child, F., (1886) *The English and Scottish Popular Ballads*

Cochrane, D., (2018) *Changeling the Lost*

Conway, D., (2002) *Moon Magic*

Cromek (1810) *Remains of Nithsdale and Galloway Song*

Daimler, M., (2019) *"Evolution of the Fairy Courts: from Scottish Ballads to Urban Fantasy"* Ohio State University Fairies and the Fantastic Conference

— (2019) *"Unseely to anti-hero: The Evolution of Dangerous Fairies in Folklore, Fiction, and Popular Belief"* Hertfordshire University's 'Ill Met By Moonlight' conference

— (2023) *"Deviance and the Liminal: fairies as justification for social subversion"* Brown University's Norm and Transgression in the Fairy-Tale Tradition: (Non)Normative Identities, Forms, and Writings conference

— (2023) "Selling Your Soul to the Fairy Queen: witches and fairies in 17th century Scotland" Witchcraft and the Supernatural in Belief, Practice, and Depiction conference

— (2024) "Tenants of Hell: Fairies, the Devil, and Folk Belief in Early Modern Scotland" Devils and Justified Sinners conference

Dalyell, J., (1801) *Scottish Poems of the Sixteenth Century*

Dansky, R., Campbell, B., Cassada, J., and Lemke, I., (1997) *Changeling the Dreaming; White Wolf second edition*

Davies, S., (2007) *The Mabinogion*

DSL (2024) *Dictionary of the Scots Language*

Dwelly, E., (1967) *The Illustrated Gaelic-English Dictionary*

Foster, M., and Tolbert, J., (2016) *The Folkloresque: Reframing Folklore in a Popular Culture World*

Goodare, J and McGill, M., ed (2020) *The Supernatural in Early Modern Scotland*

Gow, K., (2012) How Fiction Impacts Fact: The Social Impact of Books. Retrieved from https://www.fastcompany.com/1842370/how-fiction-impacts-fact-social-impact-books

Gray, S., (2014) *Dungeon Master's Guide* 5th *edition*

Hall, A., (2007). *Elves in Anglo-Saxon England*

Hamilton, L., (2000) *A Kiss of Shadows*

Harms, D., Clark, J., and Peterson, J., (2015) *The Book of Oberon*

Henderson, L., (1997) *The Guid Neighbours: Fairy Belief in Early Modern Scotland, 1500 -1800*

Henderson, L., & Cowan, E., (2007) *Scottish Fairy Belief*

Hierarchy Structure (2018) The Royal Court retrieved from https://www.hierarchystructure.com/royal-court-hierarchy/

Howard, C., (1995) *Nobles: The Shining Host for Changeling the Dreaming*

Hughes, B., (2014) *Demon Lovers: Embracing the Monster in Paranormal Romance*

Hume, P., (1629) The Flyting Betwixt Montgomerie and Polwart. Retrieved on 5 August, 2024, from https://quod.lib.umich.edu/e/eebo/A03840.0001.001/1:3?rgn=div1;view=fulltext

James I (1924) Daemonologie. Retrieved from https://archive.org/details/kingjamesfirstdm00jame

Jamieson, J., (1808) *An Etymological Dictionary of the Scottish Language*

Jamieson, R., (1806) *Popular Ballads and Songs*

Jones, M., (2024) Culhwch ac Olwen. Retrieved from https://www.ancienttexts.org/library/celtic/ctexts/culhwch.html

Kestrel, G., and Price, F., (2002) Seelie and Unseelie Courts. Retrieved from https://web.archive.org/web/20161101074718/http://archive.wizards.com/default.asp?x=dnd/fey/20021213a

Kirk, R., and Lang, A., (1893) *The Secret Commonwealth of Elves, Fauns, and Fairies*

Kirk, R., and Warner, M., (2007) *The Secret Commonwealth of Elves, Fauns, and Fairies*

Kruse, J., (2021) *How Things Work In Faery*

Lackey, M., (1992) *Born To Run*

Lyle, E., (1970). 'The Teind to Hell in Tam Lin'. Folklore Vol. 81, No. 3 (Autumn, 1970), pp. 177-181

Lyle, E., (1996). *Andrew Crawford's Collection of Ballads and Songs*

Maas, S., (2015) *Court of Thorns and Roses*

MacNeill, M., (1964) *The Festival of Lughnasa*

Magliocco, S., (2018). *'"Reconnecting to Everything": Fairies in contemporary Paganism'*, Fairies, Demons, and Nature Spirits: 'Small Gods' at the Margins of Christendom ed by Michael Ostling

Magliocco, S., (2019) *'The Taming of the Fae: Literary and Folkloric Fairies in Modern Paganism'*, Magic and Witchery in the

Modern West: Celebrating the Twentieth Anniversary of 'Triumph of the Moon' ed by Shai Feraro and Ethan Doyle White.

Matthews, J., (2006) *The Sidhe: Wisdom From the Celtic Otherworld*

McNeill, F., (1956) *The Silver Bough*

McNeil, H., (2001). *The Celtic Breeze*

Menadue, C., and Cheer, K., (2017) Human Culture and Science Fiction: A Review of the Literature. 1980 – 2016. Retrieved from https://journals.sagepub.com/doi/10.1177/2158244017723690

Miller, J., (2004). *Magic and Witchcraft in Scotland*

Murray, A., (2024) personal communication 11 August 2024

Murray, J., (1918) *The Romance and Prophecies of Thomas of Erceldoune*

Murray, J., (1872) The Complaynt of Scotlande. Retrieved on 4 August 2024 from https://archive.org/details/complayntofscotl01henruoft/page/n9/mode/2up

'On Good and Bad Fairies' (1819) The Edinburgh Magazine and Literary Miscellany. Retrieved from https://www.google.com/books/edition/The_Edinburgh_magazine_and_literary_misc/4NsEAAAAQAAJ?hl=en&gbpv=1

Pattie, T., (2011) Medieval People, Titles, Trades, and Classes. Retrieved from http://go.vsb.bc.ca/schools/templeton/departments/socialstudies/MsRamsey/Documents/Medieval%20People.pdf

Puchner, M., (2018) How Stories Have Shaped the World. Retrieved from https://www.bbc.com/culture/article/20180423-how-stories-have-shaped-the-world

Richardson-Read, S., (2015) The Good, the Dead, and the Fairy Faith: Animism and Ancestors in Scottish Folklore. Retrieved from https://cailleachs-herbarium.com/2015/12/the-good-the-dead-and-the-fairy-animism-and-ancestors-in-scottish-folklore/

— (2017) Who The Hell Is Sidhe? Retrieved from https://cailleachs-herbarium.com/2017/04/who-the-hell-is-sidhe-fairy-faith-and-animism-in-scotland-a-challenge-to-divinity/

Sands, Brymer, Murray, and Cochran, (1819) The Edinburgh Magazine and Literary Miscellany, vol. 83

Sargent, C., (1992) *Monster Mythology*

Scott, W., (1802). *Minstrelsy of the Scottish Borders*

Scott, W., (1820). *The Abbott*

Scott, W., (1831) *Letters on Demonologie and Witchcraft*

Simek, R., (1993) *Dictionary of Northern Mythology*

Simina, D., (2023) *Where Fairies Meet: Parallels Between Irish and Romanian Fairy Traditions*

— (2024) Personal communication 20 November 2024

Spangler, D., (2014) *Conversations with the Sidhe*

— (2017) *Engaging With The Sidhe: Conversations Continued*

Starling, M., (2024) *Welsh Fairies*

Thoms, W., (1884) *The Book of the Court: Exhibiting the History, Duties, and Privileges of the English Nobility and Gentry*

Walsh, B., (2002) *The Secret Commonwealth and the Fairy Belief Complex*

Weston, J., (1914) *The Chief Middle English Poets*

Wilby, E., (2005) *Cunningfolk and Familiar Spirits: Shamanistic Visionary Traditions in Early Modern British Witchcraft and Magic*

— (2010). *The Visions of Isobel Gowdie: Magic, Witchcraft and Dark Shamanism in Seventeenth-Century Scotland*

Wimberley, L., (1965) *Folklore in the English and Scottish Ballads*

Woodworth, P., (1998) *The Shining Host*

— (2001) *The Shining Host: a Player's Guide*

Young, S., (2016) In Search of the Earliest Fairy Wings Retrieved from http://www.strangehistory.net/2016/12/17/search-earliest-fairy-wings/

Young, S., (2017) The Fairy Census, Fairyist.com Retrieved from http://www.fairyist.com/wp-content/uploads/2014/10/The-Fairy-Census-2014-2017-1.pdf

About the Author

Morgan Daimler is a witch who has been a polytheist since the early '90's. Following a path inspired by the Irish Fairy Faith blended with neopagan witchcraft. Morgan teaches classes on Irish myth and magical practices, fairies, and related subjects in the United States and internationally. Morgan has been published in multiple anthologies as well as in Witches and Pagans magazine, and Pagan Dawn magazine, and she is one of the world's foremost experts on all things Fairy.

Pagan Portals (Celtic)
Lugh
Brigid
Aos Sidhe
The Dagda
The Morrigan
Irish Paganism
Raven Goddess
Manannán mac Lir
Gods and Goddesses of Ireland
Celtic Fairies in North America

Pagan Portals (Fairy)
Living Fairy
Fairy Queens
Fairy Witchcraft
21st Century Fairy

Pagan Portals (Norse)
Odin
Thor
Freya

Other Moon Books

Paid with a Kiss

Pantheon – The Irish

Pantheon – The Norse

Travelling the Fairy Path

A New Dictionary of Fairies

Fairies A Guide to the Celtic Fair Folk

Fairy – The Otherworld by Many Names

Tales of the Tuatha De Danann, Volume 1

Fairycraft – Following the Path of Fairy Witchcraft

Where the Hawthorn Grows – An American Druid's reflections

MOON BOOKS

PAGANISM & SHAMANISM

What is Paganism? A religion, a spirituality, an alternative belief system, nature worship? You can find support for all these definitions (and many more) in dictionaries, encyclopaedias, and text books of religion, but subscribe to any one and the truth will evade you. Above all Paganism is a creative pursuit, an encounter with reality, an exploration of meaning and an expression of the soul. Druids, Heathens, Wiccans and others, all contribute their insights and literary riches to the Pagan tradition. Moon Books invites you to begin or to deepen your own encounter, right here, right now.

If you have enjoyed this book, why not tell other readers by posting a review on your preferred book site.

Bestsellers from Moon Books
Pagan Portals Series

The Morrigan
Meeting the Great Queens
Morgan Daimler
Ancient and enigmatic, the Morrigan reaches out to us. On shadowed wings and in raven's call, meet the ancient Irish goddess of war, battle, prophecy, death, sovereignty, and magic.
Paperback: 978-1-78279-833-0 ebook: 978-1-78279-834-7

The Awen Alone
Walking the Path of the Solitary Druid
Joanna van der Hoeven
An introductory guide for the solitary Druid, The Awen Alone will accompany you as you explore, and seek out your own place within the natural world.
Paperback: 978-1-78279-547-6 ebook: 978-1-78279-546-9

Moon Magic
Rachel Patterson
An introduction to working with the phases of the Moon, what they are and how to live in harmony with the lunar year and to utilise all the magical powers it provides.
Paperback: 978-1-78279-281-9 ebook: 978-1-78279-282-6

Hekate
A Devotional
Vivienne Moss
Hekate, Queen of Witches and the Shadow-Lands, haunts the pages of this devotional bringing magic and enchantment into your lives
Paperback: 978-1-78535-161-7 ebook: 978-1-78535-162-4

Bestsellers from Moon Books

Keeping Her Keys
An Introduction to Hekate's Modern Witchcraft
Cyndi Brannen
Blending Hekate, witchcraft and personal development together to create
a powerful new magickal perspective.
Paperback: 978-1-78904-075-3 ebook 978-1-78904-076-0

Journey to the Dark Goddess
How to Return to Your Soul
Jane Meredith
Discover the powerful secrets of the Dark Goddess and transform your depression, grief and pain into healing and integration.
Paperback: 978-1-84694-677-6 ebook: 978-1-78099-223-5

Shamanic Reiki
Expanded Ways of Working with Universal Life Force Energy
Llyn Roberts, Robert Levy
Shamanism and Reiki are each powerful ways of healing; together, their power multiplies. Shamanic Reiki introduces techniques to help healers and Reiki practitioners tap ancient healing wisdom.
Paperback: 978-1-84694-037-8 ebook: 978-1-84694-650-9

Southern Cunning
Folkloric Witchcraft in the American South
Aaron Oberon
Modern witchcraft with a Southern flair, this book is a journey through the folklore of the American South and a look at the power these stories hold for modern witches.
Paperback: 978-1-78904-196-5 ebook: 978-1-78904-197-2

Readers of ebooks can buy or view any of these bestsellers by clicking on the live link in the title. Most titles are published in paperback and as an ebook. Paperbacks are available in traditional bookshops. Both print and ebook formats are available online.

Find more titles and sign up to our readers' newsletter www.collectiveinkbooks.com/paganism

For video content, author interviews and more, please subscribe to our YouTube channel.

MoonBooksPublishing

Follow us on social media for book news, promotions and more:

Facebook: Moon Books

Instagram: @MoonBooksCI

X: @MoonBooksCI

TikTok: @MoonBooksCI